THE SELECTED SHEPHERD
REGINALD ✳ SHEPHERD

PITT POETRY SERIES

Terrance Hayes

Nancy Krygowski

Jeffrey McDaniel

Editors

THE SELECTED SHEPHERD
REGINALD  SHEPHERD

SELECTED & WITH AN INTRODUCTION BY ✳ JERICHO BROWN

UNIVERSITY OF PITTSBURGH PRESS

Published by the University of Pittsburgh Press, Pittsburgh, Pa., 15260

Copyright © 2024, University of Pittsburgh Press

All rights reserved

Manufactured in the United States of America

Printed on acid-free paper

10 9 8 7 6 5 4 3 2 1

ISBN 13: 978-0-8229-4821-6

ISBN 10: 0-8229-4821-4

Cover photo by Robert Giard

Cover design by Alex Wolfe

CONTENTS

✳ **WRONG** ✳

☀ OTHERHOOD ☀

☀ FATA MORGANA ☀

✳ RED CLAY WEATHER ✳

INTRODUCTION

JERICHO BROWN

HOWEVER NECESSARY IT IS TO INTRODUCE READERS TO A DEAD MAN, the effort feels impossible since you mean to honor him knowing that you cannot present him as he might present himself. Like his work, Reginald Shepherd was, by all accounts, never predictable. He was brilliant, a man who seemed to have read all the books you keep meaning to read. He must have understood this about himself, and at a time when aesthetic differences in American poetry were almost violent, he never shied away from a fight or minded starting one if the fight was about the artform he loved more than he loved to "watch music videos . . . where at least one sometimes gets glimpses of shirtless guys with six-pack abs." As far as Shepherd was concerned, he had the whole of English-language poetry on his side and on the side of his poems. Why not fight? Why not write a little more wildly every time you make a new book?

In the essay—originally a blog post from early 2007—where he offers this vision of shirtless men, he also writes:

> In the perennially popular "death of poetry" discourse, there's a consensus that people don't read poetry because it's too hard, too "elitist" (another word that should be expunged from the English language: it's never descriptive, only pejorative). I've always thought the opposite, that most poetry isn't hard enough, in the

sense that it's not interesting or engaging enough. It doesn't hold the attention—you read it once or twice and you've used it up. That engagement I look for and too often miss is a kind of pleasure, in the words, the rhythms, the palpable texture of the poem. It's the opposite of boredom."[1]

Shepherd continues to elucidate and extol the benefits of difficulty in poetry, and I think the best way to introduce this volume is to say that you are holding in your hands poems that are indeed "hard enough." The question for poetry readers, the question Shepherd had for his readers, is whether or not you, too, are hard enough. Do you come to the poem to do the mind-work it asks such that by its last line you might experience the delight of having been made uncomfortable? Or are you reading to see reaffirmed in lines what you already thought you knew?

I was around twenty-four years old when I first read Reginald Shepherd's poem "Semantics at 4 P.M." in an edition of the *Best American Poetry* edited by Rita Dove. I read the poem and phoned an older and published poet I knew and said in a most accusing voice for which I should probably now apologize, "Hey, who is Reginald Shepherd, and why haven't you told me about him?" Later in that conversation, I also found a way to ask, "Well is he gay?" The poem itself does not identify its speaker as gay, but if there is a queer voice, I believed I was reading it. By turns sassy, ecstatic, elegant, and cosmopolitan in its knowledge, that voice is what led to me reading every book and essay the man wrote. That voice sounds like these lines from "A Man Named Troy" in *Angel, Interrupted*:

---

1. Reginald Shepherd, "On Difficulty in Poetry," *Writer's Chronicle*, May / Summer 2008.

> . . . Here is
> some blond man stalled halfway down a slope
> called realism in a long white car. It's called
> America, where all the accidents
> Are built to last, where all the alabaster
> And chipped marble anyone could ever use
> Is quarried and carried away.

He was a gay, Black poet who was alive. And many of the other ones I loved were dead. He was not Carl Phillips, and he was not Forrest Hamer. So, there was yet another one of us out there, and I needed to know what the hell he was doing if I was ever going to figure out what the hell I was going to do.

While that voice is an unmistakable mark of all of Shepherd's work, his poems' concerns, too, seem to be consistent in every book. These concerns can be divided into three categories. In each book, Shepherd reflects the beauty of the natural world through an understanding of that world as endangered. In his first book, *Some Are Drowning*, this endangerment appears in direct proportion to the fact of whiteness:

> . . . My true love's eyes
> are nothing like my own, are bland as the suburban lawn
> he mows on a summer Sunday afternoon, backyard
> cookout with domesticated dog. (And the beef cattle
> graze x world? And the deforestation proceeds by x miles
> per minute?")

And that endangered status matters all the more as environmental elements often get presented as characters with agency. Here are a few lines from "Surface Effects in Summer Wind" from *Wrong*:

I'm learning to remember the sound
days make: one sky disdaining the idea
of clouds, sunlight surviving
its centrifuge, breeze keeping blessed September
at bay.

And a few lines later:

> . . . Midnight,
> look at the things I've done
> in your name, in my dark, walking out
> into the street that changes nothing . . .

The second concern of Shepherd's work—and maybe the concern that we can take to be his muse—is his grief over his mother who died when he was fourteen. Shepherd's mother seems to be the trigger for much of the popular and soul music that appears in his poems, featuring figures like Donny Hathaway, Barry White, Otis Redding, and Sam Cooke. His mother's presence in poems also allows for writing about his own childhood and how he grew up in housing projects in the Bronx in New York City. She is often characterized not just as a Black woman but as a source of Blackness. Here are a few lines from "My Mother Was No White Dove" from *Red Clay Weather*:

> no dove at all, coo-rooing through the dusk
> and foraging for small seeds
> My mother was the clouded-over night
> a moon swims through . . .

And

> My mother was the murderous flight of crows
> stilled, black plumage gleaming
> among black branches, taken
> for nocturnal leaves . . .

And

> My mother always falling
> was never snow, no kind
> of bird, pigeon or crow

Years before in *Fata Morgana*, Shepherd writes of his mother, "Your body of brackish water, / black, opaque, impossible to see through // to the bottom . . ."

The final major concern of Shepherd's writing—a feature that I remember causing confusion and division when his name came up in conversations about poetry and poets—is his real life erotic desire and love for white men. There are many Black poets and other poets of color who are in sexual relationships with white people, and some of them have written about this experience. But I can't think of any other poet in history who uses the poems themselves to figure out and discover how and why he became, as he refers to himself in a 1998 interview with Charles Rowell for *Callaloo*, "a snow queen":

> ROWELL: . . . Do you continue to write about white men whom you consider to be beautiful in your forthcoming volume, *Wrong*? Because your detractors would say that you are obsessed with white men.
>
> SHEPHERD: Well, there would be some truth to that.
>
> ROWELL: What does that mean?

SHEPHERD: Well, on the most basic level it means I'm a snow queen. On a more interesting level it means that Socrates and Lacan, among others, have told us that desire is an activity within a lack. One desires what one does not have, one desires what one is not. Desire is the mark, the wound, of that lack. So I feel my own desire to be a particular case of a general fact, since obviously to be a black person who desires white people is to desire something that one is not. . . . I think that everyone suffers from this existential wound, which is simplified and reduced by being identified with being black, because though everyone in capitalist society is damaged, in a racist society to be black is to be psychologically damaged as such, and to be marked as damaged. So for a black person the universal experience of that existential wound, of the lack that constitutes the self, can be easily labeled and accounted for. "Because I am black, or because I am a person accounted for as black by a racist society, therefore I have suffered this psychic wound." Certainly I can look at white, middle-class people, people in my neighborhood, for example, because I live in a gay, hipster, yuppie neighborhood of men who are very put together and attractive, very polished in their self-presentation, and I can think these men look whole and complete, they look to be one with their bodies. I've always had a sense of distance from my body, of not being at home in my body, and again, blackness is an easy label to put on that feeling, an easy way to account for that feeling.[2]

Yes, of course, as a forty-six-year-old queer Black man with a promiscuous past (prayerfully present and future!) who has never slept with a white guy, I wonder how this "lack" Shepherd cites might be appearing in my own life since it hasn't appeared in the

2. Charles H. Rowell, "An Interview with Reginald Shepherd," *Callaloo* 21, no. 2 (Spring 1998): 298.

way that it did in his. And Shepherd uses the poems to wonder
at this lack too. In one poem, Shepherd declares the desire for:

> . . . something
> my own to sing? And not to live by white men's
> myths (not to reject those too-clear eyes, but not
> to long for them, or see through their blue distances
> all colors but my own) . . .

A few books later, in *Wrong's* "Nights and Days of Nineteen-
Something," a poem I find wholly original and quite gorgeous,
Shepherd glories in the fact of the white body:

> . . . Pink petals
> of an asshole opening under tongue,
>
> pink cockhead swollen to bursting
> purple balloon. It caught in the trees.

And a few lines later, he writes:

> . . . I never wanted him
> to ask anything of me but *suck my big*
>
> *white cock.* I come home sticky with
> his secrecies, wash them all
> off. You were my justice, just my means
> to sex itself, end justified by the mean
>
> size of the American penis. . . .

Whew! Shepherd is always clear about the troubles made by
whiteness and about the fact that whiteness always arrives wear-

ing empire and capitalism as its clothes. That clarity is all the more complex and fraught with the fact that he is also always clear about his desire (I want to write his Black desire) for white men.

I write about voice and concern because they are consistent throughout Shepherd's poems. (Another constant is the use of classical allusion and Greek myth. In a good few poems over the course of his career, Shepherd seems to identify with Orpheus— and sometimes Narcissus too. But so does the poet Terrance Hayes. These kinds of allusions in a poet's oeuvre are ubiquitous. Of course, non sequitur leaps are also ubiquitous, but Shepherd's unyielding use of them probably has a lot to do with why he was thought of as "difficult.") What changes in each book are Shepherd's poetics, his influences, his thinking about the line, line length, and line break, his use of rhyme, his approach to craft, and his rebellion against assumptions about craft.

Some Are Drowning and *Angel, Interrupted*, for instance, are Whitmanian in their long lines and litanies. In the transition from one to another, Shepherd wanted to find out more about how much a poem can hold, so the poems in *Angel, Interrupted* are the longest of his career. Much of *Otherhood* is comprised of poems in parts and a heighted use of fragmentation *because* those poems are in parts. Both *Otherhood* and *Fata Morgana* are Stevensian in nature, and they seem to be written under the influence of Modernist poetics:

> Special instructions
> to the spinner of webs, the knotter
> of strings, the weaver
> of cloth, the plaiter of nets,
> the thrower of ropes
> over chasms, special instructions
> to the builder of bridges,
> the stitcher of wounds and torn skin . . .

Red Clay Weather, published posthumously and composed in his very last days, contains the first prose poems written by a man who, up to that point, was clearly enamored with the line.

Organizing this volume and selecting its poems was a matter of tracking these shifts and idiosyncrasies such that the reader might have an experience in a single book that I had over the course of six books. I always looked forward to the next Reginald Shepherd collection because I wanted to know what he was thinking—not about grief or desire but about poetry itself. I wanted to know how his poems would refute and expand the practices of his earlier work. And I wanted to know what poetic devices he was now using as a guide or a challenge. The poems are in the same order as they are in his books, and the books are in the same order they were published. Of course, I hope these selections lead to a wider reading of these six books in full. And I hope that other Shepherd fans will read this book and be upset enough about poems I couldn't include that they post them and teach them and promote the books where they are included.

We live in a world I do not think any of us imagined in 2008 when Reginald Shepherd died, a world that would indeed make so much more possible for him. But we know poets don't die. And if they do, people who love poetry can always resurrect them. Or as Shepherd himself might say:

> The minutes continue their shine, the shapes
> of color change and turn; a wind
> blows through my skin
> and you renew the weather.
> I will not entirely die.

THE SELECTED SHEPHERD
REGINALD ✳ SHEPHERD

SOME ARE DROWNING

The Difficult Music

I started to write a song about you, then I decided, *No*.
I've been trying to write about violence
for so long. (You were my mother; I love you more
dead. Not a day goes by when I'm not turning someone
into you.) A week of traffic jams and fog
filtered through glass, the country crumbling
in my sleep; old men in plaid jackets on the corner
drinking quart bottles of Old Milwaukee; the color black
again and again.
           My first summer in Boston
a bum glanced up from tapping at the pavement with a hammer
to whisper *Nigger*, laughing, when I walked by.
I'd passed the age of consent, I suppose;
my body was never clean again. In Buffalo, a billboard
said, "In a dream you saw a way to survive and you woke up
happy," justice talking to the sidewalk on Main Street;
I thought it was talking to me, but it was just
art. (I've wronged too many mornings hallucinating
your voice, too drunk with sleep to understand
the words.)
          Some afternoons
I can see through a history of heart attacks in two-room
tenement apartments, writing your silted name
on snow with which the lake effect shrouds
a half-abandoned rust belt city. (I've compared you
to snow's unlikely predicates, the moon's
faceless occupation. Some drift
always takes your place.) I was just
scribbling again. *Take it from me*, my stereo claims, *some day*

we'll all be free. If anyone should ever write that song.
The finely sifted light falls down.

The New World

This is the paradise of emptiness, I said,
and journeyed into faithless terra incognita,
the muscles of his stomach on display
when he wipes his face with his shirt.
Or is that the charted territory,
specular fiction foreign as luxury? The trade
winds blow desultorily in this sargasso, the cargoes
of surplus value rot: salt and sable and silver,
slaves thrown overboard to reach the new world.
Today I ply the unassuming artifice
of streets and residences, walls
against a wilderness that surmounts the bricks.
His stomach, peaks of nipples
briefly glimpsed before the cotton field unfolds,
is the romantic, the failure of imagination.
The given jungle overwhelms recent settlement
after the slavers' raids; ships sink
in sight of shore. The labors of the possible
yield strict nourishment from harsh clay,
surrounded by the semiotic underworld
of palms and discontent, the rustled sibilance
of babbled and luxuriant mockery: caught up
in that extravagance, I am becoming
him, blank-eyed temptation, my jungle.
The cannibals descending on the cultivated fields
with spears, the repetitions of the unforeseen catastrophe:
that boy won't comprehend these lines. Who underwrites
his blond and vacant beauty, hatted for the hunt?
Setting out upon the voyage for the new, one comes upon

the well-mapped coast, Atlantis dripping in noon light
after the flood, and orichalcum instead of gold.
I have already misplaced his name:
there is no new world.

Slaves

These are the years of the empty hands. And what
were those just past, swift with the flash of alloyed hulls
but carrying no cargo? Outside our lives, my mythical
America, dingy rollers fringed with soot deposit
cracked syringes and used condoms on beaches tinted gray
by previous waves, but when an hour waits just for a moment,
everything begins again. All of it is yours, the longed-for
mundane: men falling from a cloud-filled sky like flakes of snow
onto the ocean, your mother immersed in ordinary misery
and burning breakfast, still alive in the small tenement
kitchen. You understand I use the second person
only as a marker: beyond these sheltered bays are monsters,
and tarnished treasures of lost galleons
it's death to bring to light. The ships put out
and they sink; before the final mast descends, the shadow
of a single sailor is burned across the sun, then wrapped
in strands of cirrus, his European skin a gift
to the black and unknown ocean floor. Of the slaves
thrown overboard to save the ship, no words
remain. What memorials the public beach becomes
in late October, scattered with Puerto Rican families
on muddied sand still lighter than a black man's
pound of flesh: it abrades my skin. I can't touch
that perfected picture of myself, no white wave
will wash either hand clean. There is a wind
riding in on the tainted waves, and what it cannot
make whole it destroys. You would say that all along
I chose wrong, antonyms of my own face
lined up like buoys, but there is another shore

on the far side of that wind. Everything is there,
outside my unhealed history, outside my fears. I
can see it now, and every third or fourth wave is clear.

Paradise

I don't know the names of flowers, or the various
songs of birds, what to call the water
falling from the sky all week, sleet or hail,
the histories of high achievement while my
great-grandparents were hidden among the cotton,
slaves. (I know what to call asphalt
slick with rain, but not the parts of that plant
that shredded their fingers.) *Thou bringest home
all things day scattered*, but let the lost, this once,
bury the lost. So much stolen that was free
for the asking. . . . Let the mutilated days sort out
their own. Swallow, swallow, when shall I
be like the swallow, singing the rape
of my voice, but singing past the rape, something
my own to sing? And not to live by white men's
myths (not to reject those too-clear eyes, but not
to long for them, or see through their blue distances
all colors but my own), or drown in that exhaustion
of hyacinth and narcissus mown down. I don't know
names of flowers, though I can mimic
those who do, the open secret of a man
who doesn't look like me, who looks like me
if I could speak my name, if I could stop
the repetitions of oppressive beauties
not my own. (I don't trust beauty anymore,
when will I stop believing it?) Skylark, I don't know
if you can find that paradise, or lead me to
the blackened ruins of my song.

The Lucky One

The middle-aged white man in a beat-up blue Pinto
who shouts "Hey man, what's up?," pulls up onto
the curb in front of me to ask the time, because
I am a young black man and who knows what he wants
from me: or my dream in which nothing works, not even the lights,
because it's France under the Occupation, and Billie Holiday
sings "I Cried for You" with blue hair on the television
while men in drag fan-dance behind her and young people
grind together in Technicolor on the studio dance floor (when the camera
isn't closing on her pancaked face, her one
gardenia pinned back like blue-rinsed hair), because the Nazis
still allow it and pleasure is such a pretty thing
to watch, and I am hiding in this house with air-conditioning, waiting
for the owners, whom I haven't met, to come home, the lights
to come back on, waking up afraid (just after
they return, turn off a dead black woman's tears)
in the second half of the twentieth century not knowing
the time of day, speaking French to myself, singing.

Sappho's Fragment Thirty-One Revised

What does the white page learn? And the words
that left their footprints there? I don't know
Greek.
   He's too much like a god, the man
with carefully combed-back hair who sits beside me
in the library. He doesn't speak.
And if he did? The white page wants

the breath's extinction; the sentence
wants an end to talk. I've spent a lifetime's
silences, spent hours on dead languages,
another century's broken English

pieced together. *To Carthage then I came . . .*
And there wove him a song, set words in soundless
lines on cotton bond. I put his blue eyes there
where they will keep (unless I throw that crumpled

text away). One man to stand for
history, asleep between clean sheets
of snow, fields of smudged and trampled-over
immortality. The words are orphans

there, drifts in recirculated air, his breath
almost mingled with mine. The eye
stepping so lightly won't recognize
itself, some draft of conversation canceled.

I leave the reading room to silence that becomes
him, walk into this unlit page he'll never read.

Two or Three Things I Know About Him

He is in the car, he is asleep, he doesn't want
to dream. He was listening to Bach on the radio,
baroque contraption coiling in the ear, black marks on a record
no one will be punished for. Just say that he's asleep.
I can't recall his name, but if you called him he might
answer, he might wake up. He was dreaming
of Miguel, of Raphael the painter and the boy
who steps out of a painting into the street
against the light and he puts on the brakes just
in time. He doesn't want to break beauty
just yet, though the boy is screaming at him and they are both
afraid. He still believes the promise of happiness by art, violence
posed as poise: a frat boy with a perfect nose who'll break
his neck. I mean to write, *That happiness is conscripted
corpses, contras and Colombian cartels, financed
from Washington.* All that happens is boys and flowers,
anemones and Enriqués, florid sexual organs
bursting forth in May to dazzle and wither
by August, wearing shorts: some puerile parable
a child could smear with paint-by-number fingerprints.
This is no discourse for adults; someone's always crashing
in the same used blue car. He is sleeping in the car
careening down the hill and hits Miguel, the impact
kills them both. He is caught inside the steering wheel
like a pigeon in the tires, he is turning
in the spokes. He has found another shape.
I've forgotten how to write his name,
I've murdered him. I know he's not asleep.

Kindertotenlieder

After midnight everything becomes musical
like the names of flowers: names of diseases, for
example, like pneumocystis

carinii pneumonia blossoming in your lungs,
its petals of infection closing the breath. I wouldn't want
to make that beautiful, a self-congratulating sadness

in my blood. There are numbers of flowers
suitable for funerals whose names I don't know, many
of them toxic if ingested. Rinse the affected area

thoroughly with cold water, irrigate
the blood: surely something will grow there, something
has to. The body is surely no grave. Like

Kaposi's sarcoma, harsh syllables pronounced
across the skin, the purple lesions almost
hyacinth. No death is quite so flower-like, the god (who was

in love, remember) turning away so not to spoil the composition.
From that boy's blood a single flower sprang; the gardens
of Adonis wither within a week. I hate

the stupid flowers stealing youth. Beauty
is not an infection, contagion is no bloom upon the cheek, the thorn
that takes the rose into the true. The death

of beauty is diagnosed by no flower. How afraid I am
of your outstretched hand, its petals
white and black and falling fingers.

Two Boys Glimpsed in Late Light

I'm finally tired of innocence, the old world
of blue-eyed boys. What if I weren't
to start with beauty (fixed, triumphant) (because beauty
isn't my friend, is it?), what if I were to talk
with him, boy in the library with a bandanna
around his head, boy with skin as brown
as mine? What if he isn't reading Provençal poetry, what if
he's not the meaning of the sensual world?

My true love's eyes
are nothing like my own, are bland as the suburban lawn
he mows on a summer Sunday afternoon, backyard
cookout with domesticated dog. (And the beef cattle
graze x world? And the deforestation proceeds by x miles
per minute?) I'll take the smell of burning flesh
locked in smoke-colored eyes, the honest violence
that cradles those blond lives in certainty, and closes
around a black man's throat and scrotum. (And the average
life expectancy of a black man is x years? And the percentage
who can read these lines is x?) Now I insist
on shattered glass sprinkled like early sudden snow
across his habitual pavements, his perfectly proportioned face
swimming the shards. (And my sullen desire, stupid, sudden
when he walks past, that makes me drop my pen, that interrupts
the rage? He's just a frat boy.) (So now
I insist?)

I wouldn't
want this studious boy to come to any harm; he's not
the one I mean. I wouldn't want to break
these lines in anger. (And the anxious faces of my friends,

all white, all not to blame?)
I'll walk beneath the yellow moon at dusk
and wish for him, I write these lines
for him. (And the broken glass, another skin?)

The First Farewell to Antinoüs

This blue to color it blue could only diminish, the Sound
a tarnished mirror off Rye Beach, mottled
with pleasure craft I can't afford. There never was
a beach, we were never there together; this is the last poem

with the ocean in it. That early in the season, water
too cold to swim, the shore was littered with pocket splendors
I collected: exoskeletons of horseshoe crabs
and plastic Pepsi cups, used condoms

and a broken sandal strap. You paced out lengths
of April sand, while I affected interest in tidal pools.
That man dredged from the waterlogged waves last year
revived, a matter of pounding on the heart

until it answers, a moment's resuscitation.
Your hand casual and significant in mine, a seagull's feather underfoot
for a reminder, and drifting from a neighboring radio
a Chet Baker blue, held to the boneless ear, al*most*

blue, almost you, and almost not a song at all. The sky
slowly going out while all the other couples left, saltwater blue
to cloudsack blue to black, and you asleep beside me just this once,
in public, in the dark. This is the last poem about you.

Tantalus in May

When I look down, I see the season's blinding flowers,
the usual mesmerizing and repellent artifacts:
a frat boy who turns too sharply from my stare,
a cardinal capturing vision in a lilac bush

on my walk home. I'm left to long
even for simple dangers. From the waist up
it's still winter, I left the world behind
a long time ago; waist down it's catching

up, a woodpecker out my window is mining grubs
from some nameless tree squirrels scramble over.
When I turn back it's gone, I hadn't realized
this had gone so far. (Everywhere I look

it's suddenly spring. No one asked
if I would like to open drastically. Look up.
It's gone.) Everywhere fruits dangle
I can't taste, their branches insurmountable,

my tongue burnt by frost. White boys, white flowers,
and foul-mouthed jays, days made of sky-blue boredoms
and everything seen much too clearly:
the utterance itself is adoration, kissing

stolid air. I hate every lovely thing about them.

Sunday

I made myself a myth to keep the century
entertained. Beauty is naked on the rock,
poorly paid hours consume my days and leave me
evenings and weekends. Let that be
my donation to the immigrants: listless
streetlights at two A.M., the last
night bus trolling past, no rest
in sight. The man preaching
on a cardboard packing box said, *If life is not
what we have asked, then we have not asked
enough.* In the brief respite
of a January thaw (the year's
first lie), I compared the unfurled sky
to my own carefully tended
bitterness, set foolish trees
unfolding in the Common
against black men asleep on benches
under the Sunday *Globe*. They hold
their cheap gin close, capitalism
is collecting trash in plastic bags
and blue recycling cans. Couples
walk past holding hands, happy
not to go hungry. The swan boats are chained up
for the season, beauty is stripped
in the clouds and cannot walk.
Stripped and questioned and beaten
with cow prods. The man preaching said, *Be happy
and do what you want. You are young
and life is too short not to*

do what you want. But he was
a foreigner. I am grateful
for the colored scraps of wanting
and vintage buttons given me, and keep them closed
in this cigar box. The god withers
to a cricket in a wicker cage.

Until She Returns

This is how I say it ends, Bronx County, 1978.
Packed up all my cares and woe in a plastic
garbage bag. It took an hour, maybe
less.
     I take myself into the river of salt
for pages at a time, lying for the sake of
accuracy. All that summer it was winter; I said it
for her sake.
               (For a year after she died
I dreamed of her; she came to say
she was just hiding. Death was just
a place to stay, a drift of cloud smeared half-way into
snow. I watched it fall.) (It never snowed there,
pine needles on red clay and heat-reek of the paper mill
for months. Mere decor, you might say, caves of kudzu
and no sidewalks. I missed sidewalks
most of all.) Some Thursday's drift of cloud stole forty years
in passing, and an extra for good luck. Some other spring
I'll give them back.
               Days spent
curled around a tattered name, erased: white
piss-smelling flowers, intimate
spring air against the throat, some warmth
not far enough away. My little sister said
we'll have to find another . . . ; we were named
after each other, before the fact. Who isn't her these days?
Hat boxes and a closet full of coats with fur collars,
someone to betray over and over. (The personal effects
incinerated, with no one to say

mine. I'll take the rhinestone buckles on the shoes.)
When death comes he'll be a fine young man
and I will kiss his rotten lips and find her there.
Here I go, singing low.

ANGEL, INTERRUPTED

Depth of Field

Desire is not this road of light on water
the half-moon leaves in its wake at one
A.M., white flakes of stone or snow
paving a lane between Lake Michigan
and a clearing sky. All day it was raining
or about to rain. It's not this long-necked bird
standing just off a fenced-in spit of sand
at the marina (NO FISHING WADING
OR SNAGGING BEYOND THIS POINT),
gray heron wading polluted currents
in sight of Lake Shore Drive. The eye admits
all this and more, water diffused to air
against a backdrop of falling temperatures
and rising barometric pressures. Something
can be made of anything at all, a couple fucking
with their clothes on against the hood of a red Ford,
a runner with a reflecting visor on the jogging path,
a gang of boys with baggy shorts and a boom box
dancing on the man-made rocks, no diving
or swimming allowed, but not desire.
The field of vision makes room for all these
things that aren't: desire, this information
poured through the widened lens, the light
from several sources, then just one. The boathouse
is outlined in mist behind a huddled clutch
of bobbing cabin cruisers. Passing headlights
fix rocks, dandelions, and my silhouette
against any horizon, then depart, leaving
behind rocks and weeds, my overshadowed form,

a trail of bone-white waves unchanged. Soon
the moon will take its boat out too far to be reflected
on by any body. The lake is completely still
this once, the distance filled in with visual detail
and every object perfectly clear. So much, but not
desire, caught against the items of this world.

Narcissus at the Adonis Theater

Since you don't understand, let me explain
my regard for these scenes in which I play
no part. Here I view his body's lesser secrets
at my leisure, and all the disappointments
they represent. Lover, I wrote, because there's no one
there. (To have done with the likeness
of his body, to have done with his body . . .
The orthodoxies betray me one by one, *oh yes, I must
have been blind.*) I can't read my own writing
in this half-light, my hands being otherwise
occupied. Here is an actor captive
to celluloid, oiled flesh trying to come
to some decision. Here are the lifelike
gestures, and here the light
gives way. Right now I am rehearsing
one moment I call reason (the theater
almost empty this time of day): glare of late afternoon
after the first matinee, clear white
afloat like some transparent hope
against an azo blue, and just as easily
seen through.
              Because you ask,
I'll say I have a friend like that, and I
give him your face: a kiss on a canvas screen
in the age of mechanical reproduction.
(He's worn away until he is that thin,
translucent so the life shows through.)
Scenes stolen by the flickering light
become some clear and credible idea, lucidity

spooled out like film, and then the reel
runs out. I'll pay to see the play again,
attend the moment you, pale as any mirror,
give your white skin to me.

Two Versions of Midsummer

The grass is a description but a description
of what, the light a paraphrase of light, the visual
rendition of an idea of blue white green blue
with a corner of gray where the storm is arriving. Fourth of

July at four o'clock, the park in Wicker Park a story I tell myself
about a park, one eye half-open, one eye halfclosed.
The sky half sky and half forecast of rain, a voice
I call my friend's explaining all the arguments that make up

a world, the text trees grass trees and the subway
trestle weave of a young man playing Frisbee with a white dog
and light blue shorts. He tosses her the Frisbee and she
won't let it go, a game she doesn't understand, it's hers,

it's all she's got, battered white disc he takes from her
and throws into the background merging into foreground,
object coming swiftly into view she catches in midair
while people clap. He grabs it and begins again, evading her

by letting go, young white man with right arm in full extension
this rendering of a man, white dog the meaning of a dog
that knows how to fetch. Dog day. It's muggy and a little rain
might cool this afternoon that I can keep all year, all

week, sweat on my brow and in my eyes, the salt
that sharpens error sharpening sight. Now I can barely hear
my friend. Now the young man's abandoning the scene,
a disappearing body's revising deciduous trees. White bones

partitioned into various limbs, femur, patella, tibia,
ulna and humerus parceled to packages of muscle, flexors
and extensors, pedal a ten-speed bike while his white dog keeps pace
with a mouthful of Frisbee. It's mine, I made it, summer

afternoon in Wicker Park. My arm reaches
for the receding picture of world, and then falls back
across the story of my face, unable to refute his body's
privacy. The day's all description and what is he now?

My Brother the Rain

Some sleep away the years until the headlands
thaw. Some build their sails for April's flood.
The ships put out on wheels of salt
and leave their foaming spokes behind
to shatter on black gravel. One by one they founder
and they fail; the sunken-hearted crews breathe water
like any other drowners. So you set out
in your dinghy to row by that light,
the river your note from a mutual friend:
you'll introduce yourself to the sea
in stages. Storms come to stir the swell, wind
comes churning a course toward the rocks
that could calm you like those sailors.

The rapids open onto ocean, you cannot steer
except toward true north. So you drift
without a rudder except your hand
that burns to let you know you're freezing.
(If you had no history you could wash ashore.)
You might call that current night, if night
weren't hung behind you, the backdrop
to your magic lantern of survivors clinging to a raft
in Arctic weather, if the light weren't frayed
and torn around the frame. (If you had no name
you could float like some floe.)
You lay yourself to sleep with sheets of snow,
wake to regret the morning, drifts like waves.

A Man Named Troy

Here are the homeless black men begging small coins
on the corner, and to the left are the instructive ruins
of others' wars, nine layers of rubble
struggling for the site of one lost city. Here is
some blond man stalled halfway down a slope
called realism in a long white car. It's called
America, where all the accidents
are built to last, where all the alabaster
and chipped marble anyone could ever use
is quarried and carried away. (Achilles is killed
by Apollo the butcher of heroes, who doesn't care
whose side he slaughters, doesn't recall
from one day's lethal sunlight to another: Apollo
who prophesied long life, beauty, and the love
of many men and women, then
forgot.) He wasn't born yet, somehow
he's responsible. He's just reading the paper
in an afternoon café, reading random
pages of unwritten history, his
or whose. He's history, him or me or someone
illegible, all too readable. Who wrote that, here.

And lined-up lighted windows aren't the eyes
of trains hurtling toward the underground entrance
of hell, the El looking into someone's living room
from up and out, just like the gods, who don't
take public transportation, who never look
before they leap from some whitewashed trestle
or another, with only one or two mortals

to break their fall. (Apollo fell
into the tenth year of the Trojan War, landed
atop an Anatolian trading town and the old queen
cried *Oimoi*, kneeling on the burnt ramparts
where the last missiles landed: no quarter
given, none expected. He broke
their ancient backs and walked to Rome. A god's feet
should never touch the ground.) The stars
aren't streetlights: lowered on their nylon strings
and hovering second-story window height, they just look
that way. Here are the windows looking away,
averted from the chain of cars that sideswipe them
and miss. Here is some man in a white T-shirt (a color
we collaborated on) watching a documentary, drowned out
by the clatter of passing traffic.

There were blind days a blond man's toss of head
to shake the careless hair back into place
above the half-closed sky-blue eyes (late Mediterranean
breakers beaten white against an Asian shore, late afternoon
sky shaking off slight rain) seemed the whim
of some Greek god: all force, gesture,
grace, the consecrated body with no mind
at all. *Why is there nothing in thy face?* Here
is a man (but never him) sitting by a plate glass window
as if in a museum, still life with stranger
seen through glass: Clark Street, the El scaffolding,
all of Chicago the just backdrop for this history
play: blank page I'm reading into, white text or

white skin. (Is skin burning paper, palimpsest, the written
over only, face again?) Now he's translating lines
about Achilles' wrath, white waves
folded over to expose the virtual wound.

(The mourners beg for mercy and Apollo
only shakes his perfectly formed head.)
Here are the homeless black men begging
drachmas and quarters on the corner
of this place soon to be called the new world.

He and Sleep Were Brothers

Night pays out her promenade in pallid goldenrod,
a mesh of stems and clustered blooms
fleeting as fall. Ghost lights halo
a clouded-over moon, then dissipate,
till dawn discovers me asleep at last. No one
could keep your perfect skin. I keep it
in this drawer, a page that holds the light
the way it should have been. When light left
it left its shape, an amethyst's shadow
traced on the papered-over windowsill
after a week of waiting. The sun will draw its silhouette
on any sensitive surface, anything willing
to change. I hold you in my hand,
an amethyst warm to the touch, leaving its mark
wherever the heat is greatest.
                              Look: my hands
are empty, like your strict new heart. Two boys
ran through a field of flowering timothy
and william, trailed fingers down the peeling banisters
of a house in need of paint: these memories I stole
from you. (*I put this moment here, I put
that moment . . .*) Your naked body
in the pool, the moon a pearl just out of reach: by morning
a man constrained by clothes, by talk, and too much gin.
He smiles weakly in my palm, and burns, trying
to turn away. The light loves him, but hurts him
anyway.
            Nights ago, when I was younger, I went down
searching for your glasswork smile: met the Sphinx

on the road to the city of thieves. The answer,
I said, was you, and your heart belling
in its fallen tor of bone. But she
thought I was lying: her raised palm was blank.
Read this and tell me what it says. The sun
falls out of sight like a stone in a lake
flung by a boy I never was. Leftover light
floats in your wake, white ripple in an empty pool,
white shadow on a slowly darkening page.

The Gods at Three A.M.

The foolish gods are doing poppers while they sing along,
they're taking off their white T-shirts and wiping the sweat
from their foreheads with them, the gods have tattoos
of skulls and roses on their shoulders, perhaps a pink triangle
above the left nipple, for them there's hope. The gods
are pausing to light cigarettes while they dance, they're laughing
at private jokes while the smoke machine comes on,
one of the gods told you they put talcum powder
in the artificial fog, then walked away, how could anyone
breathe talcum powder, but it makes their skin shine
with the sweat and smell of cigarettes and Obsession. Don't try
to say you didn't know the gods are always white, the statues
told you that. The gods don't say hello, and when you ask them
how they are the gods say they don't know, the gods
are drunk and don't feel like talking now, but you
can touch their muscled backs when they pass.

The gods in backwards baseball caps say
free love, they say *this is the time*, and disappear
into another corner of the bar, they're always moving
to another song. The gods with their checked flannel
shirts unbuttoned under open motorcycle jackets,
hard nipples and ghost-white briefs above the waistbands
of their baggy jeans, say *get here*, the gods say *soon*, and you just
keep dancing because you don't know the words, you hope
the gods will notice small devotions and smile, maybe
a quick thumbs-up if you're good. The gods
whose perfect instances of bodies last only
for the instant, or until last call (and then

they disappear into the sidewalk), gods who are splendid
without meaning to be, who do they need
to impress, say *this could be the magic*, they say
live for tonight, and then the lights come on.

Jouissance

And then the sky separated into frayed parts, torn
falling bits, world coming apart in my hands
into the snow I tried to piece it back together
out of, sudden snow that patched over cracks
on Halsted Street, freeze-dried dog shit and lost

single gloves pressed into the broken sidewalk
for safekeeping. There were caves under the pavement
where I couldn't find the forms, see the rats. I tried
soldering a scene together out of white, my
absence, but snow collapsed inside my palms,

left me just indented lines and street signs
someone scribbled over before my time. Another
wall whose writing I can't read, another eye
helping itself to a second portion of light.
I slipped and braced myself against a building

glazed with clear ice, no surface anywhere
that would hold. Saw my future in the bricks
of ice snow wouldn't make a landscape, flurries
irretrievably plural, intermittent, like the light,
like the glitter from smashed bottles, beer brown

and soda clear, by now parts of the pavement too.
If it stumbles again, let fingers sink
in loam leached of moisture, color: a second-story
window box, one scumbled world (a leaf, a scrap
of Styrofoam) crumbling between cold fingertips.

Black Ice on Green Dolphin Street

Why worship whiteness always, what virtue
in that candor, what quality? Face
always the same, same turning away
when you turn, same singular routine
hypothesis: one man in one posture, one world
like a relief map of the world. When he turns
you are turning from the summary glance, a little
light captured in the momentary retina, but
reversed. Forget the long discussions of the soul
you might have held while weeks fell into winter,
forget the death of Socrates, a paper cup of wisdom
spilled on linoleum. In Hesiod's *Theogony*, I'm told,
the Muses say, We are capable of making lies sound
true, but we can also tell the truth. You wander
like a blind cat through your night, first
idea of sky which weather only contradicts. Headlights
and streetlights shadowbox across the shades: you too
will never touch. How many nights
have you maintained pale skin nothing mars
(walking out past three A.M. to be convinced the true
can become beautiful), until a sleepless dawn
allows for no more stars and allegories? Algol,
Regulus, Altair, Rigel and Betelgeuse, the lights
lesser and great with Arabic or Latin names, white
dwarves and red giants, yellow main sequence
luminosities. That man and his blond cowlick live alone
in paradise with a forecast of light rain, a tenement
of token clouds against a tarp of blue felicities. Down
from the Great Rif to a barrier reef, the snow

goes where it will, and when. (*I have come from going
to and fro in the earth, and from walking up and down
in it, but I have come.*) Your winter steals the signal
flesh and ruins it, leaves limbs at broken angles
on the slope and green bottle glass
smashed into the speckled pavement: a sheer waste
of transparencies laid over midnight. It keeps
a flawed reflection of the sky, constellations
past the tree line blurred by the walking
streetlights home. The glassed-in contradictions keep
their distance, but they keep. (*You made your myth, now lie
in it.*) The body stiffens as it wakes, sheathed by a cold
window left open, the recurring dream of glaciers, lying
in its mirror. Open your hand and let it go, zero
down to less than that, and then less than what's left.
That's you. The snow begins as clouds and ends
as any water. Navy, royal, azo, aquamarine
and indigo: I've drowned too many nights
in blue. Even historical weathers leave a trace.

Drawing from Life

Look: I am building absence
out of this room's air, I'm reading suppositions into
summer's script snarled on a varnished floor.
It looks like a man. That knot's his hand
waving good-bye, that stippled stripe of grain's
the stacked-up vertebrae of his turned back.
Small birds (sparrows or finches, or perhaps)
are cluttering the trees with blackened ornaments (burning
in the remnant light of August eight o'clock), and noises
I can't hear. Chirring there, chittering. The window's closed.

I am assembling a lack of sound
in this locked box, and dotting all the i's
these floating motes present (my composition), I am not lonely
for the palpable world (midges I clap hands for
and kill), shivering into darkness underwater outside glass:
what's left of light sinking from zero down to less,
cobalt down to zaffer, deeper to purple-black
where divers drown. The swimming landscape's
all mistake (one world that shuts air into
my submerged terrarium), and I am luck.

Tornado Watch

Who was it I was saving my white kisses for?
As if it weren't my own tongue down my throat.
My amateur astronomies forgot the tearing paper bags of milk
stars carting back a summer torrent. Traffic
amplified by watered asphalt will steal my sleep
all night, the barking dog next door will drive me
to some new distraction. America, rain
soaks your skin white as bleached sheets, suffering from wind
-stripped leaves. It's raining among your various
tones of voice. I'm aspiring to a storm worth surviving.

I heard these tasseled plains were coral beds, a continental ocean
incognito, freeze-dried under your amber waves.
I heard somewhere you were a fisherman of men.
The self glimpsed through a sewer grating's grid
recedes like light behind the coalsack sky; an oil slick
eddies in a flooded gutter. *When I came to those waters
I forgot how to swim.* A puddle of mud makes a soggy
keepsake, a warning siren makes a piss-poor song.
(It's raining across your burning acres
of corn, salt lake in which troll pledges
hooked like lures. Walking on water's easy
when you're struggling on a nylon line.)

I'd like an acid rain to steep my skin
and peel the interpretations off (*wash me white
in the blood of goddamns*), time's tide
would like to slip my useless body under his arm
and carry me out like a comber. My state's too far inland

to hope for much from dilettantes. (*Will he always be arriving,*
or will you have to bring your foaming lips to his?)
I can already feel the first sprinkles of toxic soil
on my head. It's only rain, the happenstances
worn away to damp cracked streets and condensation
on the pane, nothing like real weather.

Sam Cooke Would Be Sixty-One This Year

It's always too late for the October revolutions,
failures lined up like Roman candles
in the rain. They still come around begging
for change. (So nothing works, not even disappointment's
last good nerve? So the dead letter office
returns his mail?) It's noon
all afternoon, it's well this side of yesterday
today. *A change is gonna come*, I heard sometime,

but my radio's gone dead. My best friend said
there might be work for me, my mother told me
never argue with a white man, you'll never win
that way. Not even the bus stops
wait for me. The signs have all been taken down
for repairs, no second person's loitered on that corner
in decades: I couldn't even hail a taxi
for you. Someone says "Now you're asleep"

three hundred times until I believe it. (Imagination
is a funny thing, good night Johnny Mercer. Maybe
he should ask a fucking daisy what to do.) The walls
are sweating whitewashed nails, the windows are raising
my pain threshold, I must be asleep by now.
The thick of it was summer floods and mildewed pages
stuck together, *Fuck the Proletariat*
Parts One through Four; the thin was *Freedom Through Education*

For the Negro Race. It's a black letter day
in Iowa, it's thirteen o'clock on Thursday, and *like that river
I've been running ever since.* I went out the movies, *Glory*
with Matthew Broderick as Colonel Shaw, who made men
out of a bunch of niggers, and a hailstone
hit me on the head, my little piece of heaven
or the end of fall. To tell the truth
I saw it twice, but couldn't tell you when.

A Plague for Kit Marlowe

In Memory of Derek Jarman:
"I place a delphinium, Blue, upon your grave."

I

I don't trust beauty anymore, when will I stop
believing it, repeating wilted petals? He loves
me not. Delphinium, cornflower, lupine, flowers
I've never seen: forget-me-not, fringed gentian,
lobelia, love-in-a-mist, old names of a world
that never was mine, the last of England's green
and pleasant island, sheer blue above the whited
Dover cliffs. Blue fog spelled out across an August sky
the blinded retina keeps, blue frost of a February
dawn, blue hour where you're dead. Agapanthus, also
called lily-of-the-Nile, closer to my lost continent. Pressed
in this anthology of hours, the serifed letters keep
for years of pages, film on water. Scilla, flax, large periwinkle.
Nothing is wasted but regret. Bluebell, blue flag.

II

The gardens of Adonis wither like burnt pages. Beauty
is an infection, I see now, the paper-thin skin written on water
like hyacinth, lily and anemone floating to decay. The filmy blossoms
fall apart like my hands, like *shallow rivers to whose falls*
Melodious birds sing madrigals. Narcissus was pushed, drowned in
a flood of song; Leander's white shoulder is coral echoing
the Dardanelles. *For in his looks were all that men desire.*

I tramp through a closed garden of cures, Foscarnet, Retrovir,
Zovirax, gaudy bouquets which wilt expensively
before ever reaching you. Roferon, Sporonox,
Leukine and Cytovene: those plastic flowers lose color
in the windows of a funeral home, pink wax and wire
accumulating dust like any dead. *And I will make thee*
beds of roses And a thousand fragrant posies.

III

Saw ye him whom my soul loveth? Will culture cure me, keep me
from harm? It let him die. I wanted some white immortality,
but find *I from myself am banish'd* in these lines, ghost body
of the light I poured away. My hands are stained and helpless
here, black ink spilled uselessly as any blood. The heart
is attached to a branching tree of capillaries, veins and arteries,
oxygen flowering like amaryllis, rose of Sharon, vermilion trumpets
forced in January, Sebastian's month. *Why should you love him
whom the world hates so?* The heart wants to keep opening
for seven years of any kind of luck, for any body's blood. Small bells
of paperwhite narcissus fill someone's winter with an idea of scent,
released of color, shape, or sense of touch. Who wouldn't wish
to linger in the sensual world that won't spare me, or let me hold
a living hand to him, *the king in whose bosom let me die.*

IV

I wanted something musical for you, notes floating
on the margins of a stranger's days and works: a lark, an air
of spring somewhere, my voice not clouded under error
just this once. How fine the song I wanted then,
changing from major to minor and, strangely,
back again. The knowing gods must think so little
of my minor wishes, all the sentimental tunes
I've memorized off-key: repeating every error helplessly
to make a song's my one refrain. I suppose I die
a little every day, not noticing it yet. I'm gathering dust
from an occasional shaft of light, I'm dotting all the i's
whole notes repeat, like why or cry. There's no finer tune
than afternoons clouded with luck all spring, the margin of error
I'd call a song. This happens every time I try to say good-bye.

A Little Knowledge

Take me into night, but I'm already there: something dark
in the night, something light in the day. *Red sky
at dawn, sailor be warned.* There was a winter
beach we never walked. The poems I wanted were nothing
like my heart: nothing joined us
together, nothing held us apart. Forgive me if I pretend
to speak to you, blind wind from the waves, misled.

Each day you grow easier to imagine: you look different
every time. A chipped nail on the second finger, a halo
of gold hair about the ear: none of it
adds up to you, prince of the uninhabited. Remembering
is a salt-rose at the mercy of high sprays, surge and plunge.
There is no song without remembering, but your eyes
aren't blue at all. Sailors are drowning in you.

I know where all the gathered waters burn, green star
that scatters, then retracts, its light, stippled spindrift
of sails in failing dusk. I cup that flame in my palm: black water
chars the skin, where there's no song. It casts white cities
on the walls of night, smoke clouds like galaxies, oceans
away. Something about the light
as it strikes your hair, nothing to do with you.

Narcissus and the Namesake River

It was a lie they told about Narcissus, a libel
on his name. He never loved himself, not anyone
who looked like him. Narcissus didn't know
his own profile. There were no mirrors
in those eras, just helpless echoes. He fell for
what he wanted to fall through, a man he'd never

be: that's desire, the long arm of the father's law
taxing taxonomies, order and phylum and genus and class
uprooting upstart weeds. (Weeds are just flowers before family
names, a kingdom yet to come. Narcissus never knew his
father either, never talked back, or could have doubled back
home. He planted himself unspecific on the bank.) That woman

lip-synching without a face was no help. He couldn't help but drown
in the cold swift overflow called *you*: the mainstream, not
a tributary, unruly spring displacing every basin or
floodplain. The other is a lack; the self, delusion;
and you've got to lose yourself to be found
wanting. He wasn't suffering from self-delusion, just a mistake called

identity. Narcissus would do anything to please, so
when that face half-hidden in the current (was it running
away to sea, like a sailor?) said *Kiss me, or don't come around here
anymore*, he did. The perfect kiss, of course, was death,
but who needs to fall twice? And the flower?
It only wants to be picked, cut and placed in cool still water.

WRONG

Antibody

I've heard that blood will always tell:
tell me then, antigen, declining white cell count
answer, who wouldn't die for beauty
if he could? Microbe of mine, you don't have me
in mind. (The man fan-dancing from 1978
hit me with a feather's edge across the face, ghost
of a kiss. It burned.) Men who have paid
their brilliant bodies for soul's desire, a night
or hour, fifteen minutes of skin brushed against
bright skin, burn down to smoke and cinders
shaken over backyard gardens, charred
bone bits sieved out over water. The flat earth
loves them even contaminated, turned over
for no one's spring. Iris and gentian
spring up like blue flames, discard those parts
more perishable: lips, penises, testicles,
a lick of semen on the tongue, and other things
in the vicinity of sex. Up and down the sidewalk
stroll local gods (see also: saunter, promenade,
parade of possibilities, virtues at play: Sunday
afternoons before tea dance, off-white
evenings kneeling at public urinals, consumed
by what confuses, consuming it
too). Time in its burn is any
life, those hours, afternoons, buildings
smudged with soot and city residues. Later
they take your blood, that tells secrets
it doesn't know, bodies can refuse
their being such, rushing into someone's

wish not to be. My babbling blood.
What's left of burning
burns as well: me down to blackened
glass, an offering in anthracite,
the darkest glitter smoldering underground
until it consumes the earth
which loves me anyway, I'm sure.

Deepest of the Great Lakes, Largest Too

How is this explained? First there is nothing
then there is something. Water
falls like algid dreams, like streams
of multicolored light, streamers bundled into white
that won't separate, white light repeating white
until light leaves. The lake is not a reflection
of noon, noon is no one
thing at all, noon is here and gone. The sky
is a distraction from the lake. Blue
you could hold in your hands slipping
away, spilled onto fissured concrete
and artificial sand: soaking in, vanishing. Water
reflects blue, the refraction:
on some days, green, or the imagined
Mediterranean coast. The current
is green with algae on a humid day, the lake
is alive, deep water much cooler
than air. Help the light lift up, pour out
as dusk, or cupped hands opening
clearly. Blue midnight, blue of noon.

Surface Effects in Summer Wind

I'm learning to remember the sound
days make: one sky disdaining the idea
of clouds, sunlight surviving
its centrifuge, breeze keeping blessed September
at bay. Sweet smell of short-haired boys
I try to recall, having been away from skin
for so long, some youth theirs or mine,
sprint for shelter from an August
one o'clock, heat's peak: season's
entourage with a line of sweat
kissing the shirt to the chest, a valor.
I could believe the earth itself
thought well of those domesticated
demigods, adhering to new
sidewalks in several likenesses.
So walked beside water instead.
(Dear echo, lake, repeating
wake where I find my face awash
in rocks and algae, stuttered counterpoint
of surge and current.) Midnight,
look at the things I've done
in your name, in my dark, walking out
into the street that changes nothing, littered
with leaves and cellophane, giving a little light
back, giving it away. The promised pleasure
locked in a stranger's careless body, his smell
in morning sheets; a jump of cards
in an idle man's hands, and summer ends.

Vampires

For Alvin Feinman

Nevertheless, I've been asked to write about vampires,
so I will write of the lake and its three winds: gust, gale, and blast.
Lampblack that swallows days, coal that won't shine
unless it burns. This coal withholds its heat. I'll write
lines the swan, soot and obsidian knife, draws through slow drifts,
bone-white sifting powdered mirrors over anthracite.
It's said that vampires won't cross running water,
but these waters have never moved. Lie still,
my love. The dead hone here their gift for suffering
on cold air sharp as glass shards. The swan
glides in and out of these blanched lines, its single song
a burden we taught it, this you or I or anyone, this wind.
Beneath certain cities lie the ruins of previous cities
destroyed by fire, and the bodies of the unburied dead. They wander
looking for voices between twilight and dawn, light
ticking a clock in their chests. The song they have lost
is the blood in your throat, black pinions of that swan,
snow building its white artifice against my window all long
night: cold and a knocking radiator, waiting for warmth.
This is my song for vampires, for swans
and for snow: a song, like every song, for the dead.

Hermes, the Trickster

If there must be a god in the house, let him be one
That will not hear us when we speak.
WALLACE STEVENS

Wing born of bone, tear in my sky
storm pours through, passing
through; tear in my side, my bloodshot
eye, the side heart lists to
but never sinks. These dreams
damaged in transit burn down like
tenements collapsing, unsound
slum of wishes on an occasional
evening star, Venus or unidentified object
flying blind, a common error. You
cauterize my sleep, you're part of it
by now. What else do you want
from me, except to disappear? I'd like that
too. You're knocking on my nightly
window, squall pressing full lips
to wet pane, you're grinding against
the other side of glass; they don't even
leave a print. You in your black leather
jacket and white briefs, you must be
cold, man at my window mouthing Cole
Porter, don't you know you never
can win, and I say I'm not that old. Little
fool asking for kisses, careless
trust. Careful. Heartbeat
repeating *du, du, du,* you
soundtrack of my sleep, breathe
in, breathe out, this oxygen
so pure it kills. *Don't exist,* I've asked

of you, and you've complied:
you'd like me to let you in
or let you go away. Torrents of your
almost lash cracked glass night-in, night
-out like rain, always like winter
rain in May. Avatar, sharp rib
ripped from my side, I hear your friends
calling you *little wing*.

Locale

Observe the snow: it changes
and remains the same. Single
and several at once, a manyness
of one. You find yourself in a place
and you find yourself the place, seeing

and scene, these arguments in the picture plane
where matter steps from its molds
and goes shapeless, naked of form
or ornament: discarded streetlight, brick,
horizon-line with sun falling into

purple-blue; an ochre leaf gone to gray
pavement. One night is a stone
in the mouth of sleep, heavy
and useful for building. Who is the garden
of delights, who is the light? After midnight

the men in baseball caps walk up and down
in it, tramping it deeper into sight: packing the rifts
with sleeplessness, filling the gaps
with lack. The ghosts are nude
except for their dismay, red leaves

stray back and forth across it. He was a reply
in kind, a dazzle of dying shadow
in a clock, the consciousness too adequate
to what it chooses to surrender to:
sleeping, pretending snow.

Who Owns the Night and Leases Stars

I wanted to be touched, so I went walking
at four A.M., looking for cars. (I could have
written *loved*, lake wind that late a glove

that kept my body cold, so it would keep.) Blue
was the color I chose, because of the visible
sky even then, inside the black and under

purple; occluding streetlights ticked
off every half a block or so. I walked more
than half an hour, no one was scouring

cold streets (*they are all gone into the world
of good-nights*), looking for a light or wrist
-watch. No one stopped and offered me

a ride to some room I've never been
before, or wait, I have, some neighbor
-hood, apartment, studio, some other part

of town where no one remembers my name, naked
when the lights go out. Harm is in us, and power
to harm, a stranger's hands staining my body

until I can't be found again. No one picked me
up or put me back in place, no one asked me
the time, and I told him the truth. At four A.M.

I went out walking, waiting to be touched.

That Man

For Jacqueline Lalley

I

in the green fleece shorts is taking off
his mustard shirt. There 's a T-shirt
the same color underneath. Almost the same.

No, not that one.

2

What I wanted one evening, other evenings:
the trim of honeyed skin between the yellow
and the green; glancing angle
of calf when the right heel pivots
to the left; uneven blue space the mat retains
where he has stretched. I wanted one evening
like another, air free to come and go.

(Imagine myself agraze in that green,
grace of that sexual field a meadow
where I can do no harm, rabbit
or roan oribi hurting grass. But of course
I am a predator, and fail.)

3

Now he's the world of what happens
happening, flex of thigh or twenty-degree
twist of torso, unclassical
colors still painting the skin
while he extends himself
into the overheated room. Mimesis,
the body mimicking itself, in imitation
of other bodies. Sweat and the chill
of an opened fire door, a rise of skin
where skin can't be seen.

(The branching tree of bones he is.)

4

A man in motion for once, not parts
to make a man, make up
for him. (Positions his body
assumes and discards, unwilling to be wrong
for long.) Inner of an elbow, back of
a knee (concave where I curl up
with my mirror): wherever the body bends
or turns away.

5

Soul says nothing
of consequence, over and over, says flesh
repeating itself articulately: waxy rhyme
of salvation, a self identical
with self, reflective sheen
of perspiration:
An ordinary handsome man
improving himself after work.
Thirty-four or thirty-five.
Six o'clock.

6

The lockers not the same
green as his shorts, stuccoed
with rust, matte walls a blue
when the blue has drained out, pale
and certain as an aging sky.
I'm a visitor in this new city, sky
made of spackle and cement: both of us
naked, only one nude. Then
there is no man at all.

7

The poem doesn't think of him.

Littler Sonnet

For Susan Stewart

Knot of the not forever becoming
untied, tied down there in the nowhere,
in the nevermore but this next time,
the space before that running out

exactly now, all of the exactions, all
that undone. The, the, continuing pretense
of definite identity, identifiability,
to identify, a shopworn article of

outgrown faith, no other than an an
after the end. Sound of a book, a kind
of book, a fold or a field or a forest
of pages opening, step inside

or step aside, closing all its gold leaves
at once at nightfall (night one): nature, it's said
silently (sad), is a forest of cuneiform and wooden
runes, stiff marks made on a mind

made out of paper, world made only
out of words, murmurs not mine: signs, signals,
sigils: synecdoches in an atmosphere turned inside
out, divesting moisture, flashes

of lightning through a tornado watch. That
kind of weather, kindness of whether
or not the map was accurate, acutely
read, interpreted precisely, pristine

representation of the falling
fact, traced out. Don't walk out into
a thunderstorm (it said), the flooded sky
will hail you by the wrong name, all

of them: indefinite, invisible, zero degree
of last night's next week coming. Thunder
under what happens, happening, slammed
book of closing doors disclosed, echoing

corridor. Whither your wherewithal
with words?

Nights and Days of Nineteen-Something

For Marilyn Hacker

Midsummer with other men's lovers, fumbles
on a living room couch, significance asleep
upstairs: I come through the door, I come
through the door, I came and was

conquered by tensed thighs, taut buttocks.
Asses, asses, lust from lust, a must
of sweat on matted hair, a spill of semen
down my thigh. (Classicism revised, or

what shall we do with a drunken
torso, machine shop of body parts, some
of them functional. Pink petals
of an asshole opening under tongue,

pink cockhead swollen to bursting
purple balloon. It caught in the trees.)
Who am I to think that
I'm not always on my knees

taking in some stranger strayed too far
from what he wouldn't want
to work for, paying out the line
we've always used. *Hey, do you want*

a ride? I'm walking through a field
of safety glass without my shoes; it itches,
like a sneeze. (Say it, no things but in
ideas: desire, denial; define, defiler. Decide,

then choose for me. Mother may I
go down on this man?) The tuck
in my jeans itches afterward, salt
smudge under my knees. This

is for your body made out of words,
the worse for wear if you were there, or
where I wanted me to be. *And where
were you last night, young man?* (Here's

a rumor someone passed along: I believed in
his present tense, wrapped in tinfoil and a tissue
paper ribbon, his cock worn to the right
and the several layers that kept me from it,

the shirt and several layers most of all.)
*If you have many desires your life
will be interesting*, a modernism of poverty
and stained sheets, twin bed he went to

with me, came up for air and other things.
It was never sex I wanted, the grand etcetera
with a paper towel to wipe it up. I wanted him
to talk to me about Rimbaud while

I sucked him off in the park, drunk
as any wooden boat and tasting of old cigarettes
and Bailey's Irish Cream, my juvenilia. *Don't talk
with your mouth full.* (In the clearing

at the bottom of the artificial hill, his two hands
covered every part of me until I couldn't be seen,
a darkness past the burnt-out lamppost.
We came up empty-handed. *You're so empty*

-headed sometimes.) I never wanted love
from him, his needs adhesive, clinging like
old sweat, cold sperm; I never wanted him
to ask anything of me but suck *my big*

white cock. I come home sticky with
his secrecies, wash them all
off. You were my justice, just my means
to sex itself, end justified by the mean

size of the American penis. Just keep going
that way. You'd like to sleep, you'd like to be
left alone for miles of near-misses, missteps, mirrors
in a public bathroom, all mistake

and brief apology. (My lakefront myths of you
all insufficient to the taste of come
lapping my tongue.) The jogging path
curves up into that dark place in the trees

just past the rusted totem pole. Let me
lick salt from white skin in the moon's first light
when it lies brightest: argent, ardent, concrete
and utter falsehood. Comely, my comeuppance,

comfort me: come to mind at any time,
come again for me. Take me to the boy.

OTHERHOOD

Reasons for Living

We're walking with the backwards
river, sluggish water dialects
spell out spilled lakefront's
tumbledown babble of dressed
stones, nervous dogs and "no
swimming" pictographs: the land
washes ashore with under
clinging to it, undermining
crumble, halted fall. We pick our way
to level rock, watch out for oblique
angle slabs, it's so hot
we take off our pants, we lie down
and are grass, that green
and spore-filled, well-adapted
to be carried on the wind.

Mold-colored water dulled
by use (pastel, muddled
nephrite, more common
than true jade, less highly prized,
its luster oily rather than vitreous,
a scum spilled across perspective)
with a turquoise line to build horizon
out of: prehnite, andradite,
alkali tourmaline, a seam of
semiprecious chrysoprase: anything
but true emerald, a grass-green beryl,
smaragdos, prized for medicinal
virtues: uvarovite even rarer

among garnets, its crystals typically
too small to cut.

A broken landscape (man-made)
says to its place, "I don't
remember you," unphrased,
grooved by the gaze, chiseled
into being unseen, a glancing
blow: incursions of the geometric
(cement no place to rest your head),
naked economy, awkward skin
on green towels. And then a stirring
at the other side of when,
complicit blood flows back
into the stem, in retrospect
unfinished: we stand up
erect as grass, xylem, parenchyma,
epidermis, leaf blade and sheath.

Little Hands

1

Here actors estrange themselves
from acts. Glare ladles light
across the radius, high canopies
luxuriant with epiphytes, trees
are shaken into green, drench
of wind disturbing leaves
to drunken semaphores: little
hands designing new catamites
for outmoded gods.

2

At this time every year
divinity died, the Adonis
flowed red with his blood:
clay runoff from the Lebanon.

3

Chipped singing of arrowheads
and off-white statuary scree
plowed up in a burnt west field
declining a little into afternoon
(some columns broken off
mid-thought) rings against
well-rusted blades: a waste
of monuments, miles of ravens

and manure, rivers
with the names of trees,
the Cedar flooding summer.
Rome's staple crop
was wheat—called corn—along
with barley, raised for stock
feed and some places
for beer: peas and beans
also, though forbidden
by Pythagoras. The slow
-maturing olive; figs, pome
-granates, plums; grapevines
trained on a variety of trees.

4

The man becomes a boy eventually
(blank body a white page
where wishes write themselves): shape
left behind by the sculpture wind,
but stamped with it nonetheless. Certain
human behaviors propagate gods,
nostalgia for the whole he's been
referred to: an exercise of will
around the block, through the park
and down the hill, the possibilities
still unexhausted. Some are games
and some have numbers, some
are hollow, make a ringing sound.

5

Silence, item, silence.

6

The god fucks himself with a fig branch
above the open grave, admirer
of hopeless machines—starling
pasted to the street, dysfunctional
flying contraption; the god
forsakes himself for his own sake
(pledged to slick feathers
frescoed on funerary pavement),
takes himself back to him. *Whore,*
they honor him in caves
and tearoom stalls, alleys
and temple courtyards. Color
is light's continuity, the stem
still new to the trunk, leaf
darkening to fruit, to seeds.

7

Mere world, where every man's
the artist of himself, body
his medium, interference (an inference
at most). The statues sweating, overflowing
with the fear of form, prefabricated

weather on the other side of glass:
cute guys in various states of disrepair
sighted from across the burning bridge,
and voices in salt water singing
"pale Gomorrah." I walked into my ocean,
meet me under the whale.

Periplus

The way the lake is a fact, yes: cold water
is on fire, flames
fleck off on the palm, pour out (gold sands
of the River Pactolus, King Sun
metals afternoon, gilds fingers
stiff): an occasion of light and movement
in the phenomenal world.

Knife edge of fact, contrast
so keen it draws blood: sand and fresh
water, jetty and waves subsiding
as one: a sharp pebble or glass
shard cuts bare dirty feet, infects
the body with late September.
You see that a fact
has a form, feel its imprint for weeks.

1. visible only in the event of
2. pieced into broken soil and pebbles
3. sifting the preceding absences
4. when the sun is precisely at meridian
5. oil slick in a clogged sewer grate
6. hitting tumbledown stones at such an angle
7. water not burning because already burned
8. barring any similar seasonal occurrence
9. fire, or other process of oxidization
10. _____

*

Mare Tyrrhenum
Mare Adriaticum
Mare Aegaeum
Pontus Euxinus
Mare Hyrcanium

*

Drawbridge rising over the redirected
Chicago River to let two barges
under (rusted machinery
of motion, lift and heave):
the river a massive purchase
on time, slow gallons going in reverse.

*

Things go down the North Branch
and get dirty, new words
I've no resistance to, *welter*
and *gully*, *runnel* and *mulch*,
foaming at the aeration pipes.

＊

Mare Mediterraneum
"the sea between the lands"

monsters here (whirlpools
as well, clashing rocks)

＊

Still life, still life, rows of
heaped-up dead things: starling
merging with mud and decaying weeds
by the park pond, clouds filigreed with
reflective poisons (the start
of water), a drawbridge broken over
Cermak Avenue. Monarch
glued to the broad way, one wing
perpendicular to street (orange
and black sail, flag of
convenience), one black
-furred body spilled on asphalt.

This bird that claims the morning
branch and makes the tree a factory
of song. Song scars cold air.

Burnt from the Notebooks

His boyhood loves him, clings
to his skin: pungent smell of lemons,
crushed mint and eucalyptus leaves
heal air, laurel twins verdant hair:

thinks he is myrtle, evergreen
of marriage, mourning too, carves
him out of myth and solitary
white flowers, black fruit

✳

Clove, allspice, evening primrose
where evening never calls:
he relies entirely on absence
republic of volatile oils

clearing an empty place in the mind
repeating each punctual gesture
(taking his place in the empty mind
small island of climbing vines)

✳

The god is a boy whose arrows
have been stolen, snapped
one by one by my humiliated hands

useful for kindling now

*

Sunday blush of boys cruising
crackling leaves and trash, faith in
redundancy's ruthless youth

(out looking for just a piece
of sex, torn phallic branchlet
oozing camphor, eugenol)

contingencies of shedding trees
and buildings under demolition,
construction dust of new condominiums

(as if desire had a history, came down
with clinging vines ripped from red bricks
small thorns scoring my palms)

*

Forecast clouds fold open, let go
of their resentments: rain
strips October bare

Three Songs about Snow

1

I spoke every week
into weather (wheel, hub,
axle sky with turning

vapor trails, high rises). Clouds
let go of letting go, hail sleet, snow
snares light, glare ice

by midnight. Flurried sun
a hook to hang perceptions, grapple,
pulley, hauls in salted gravel.

2

I hide myself, but am
no one, come into view
the same white

overpass, cars tossed
underhand across the lane
divider, line dividing gray

-brown field and gray
-white afternoon:
I am a dark

3

Each day almost believable
adhering to protocol:

incidents of water
at an oblique angle to air

a whole ragged silk
of torn storm

I climbed his voice
when it was cold

Les Semblables

Stringent syntax of brick dust, cracked
leaves, broken up
pavement and a dead finch, dun
feathers dusted with brick
grit, all the same
color, mine:
                  something
will be built there
I can't afford, blue sky
of your terrifying mouth,
my roof without a ceiling
leaking wind
               Adore, a door
burnt open, lintel, jamb still
standing, salvaged brick
and timber:
                  "carrying the load
above an opening"

                    Persistent drone
of sky, high tension wire, jet
contrail, drift of Canada
geese incised on clouds
cut off midshape, trailing
water particles
                 Wingspan at meridian
turned on an anecdotal wheel,
a clutch of ruined wind

Strict noon criteria, qualifying,
qualifying, when isn't a god unlucky
for his lovers

Hygiene

how do you like your blueeyed boy
Mister Death

e.e. cummings

I

Some men wash their hands five times
a day and still feel dirty. Ablutomania,
mysophobia, who can be clean
enough? *Just look at your fingernails!*
Everyone in this town's still washing his hands
of Jeffrey Dahmer, it's
1993, fifty degrees at noon
in May.
            "For a lot of black guys it's a treat
to sleep with a white man." I'm sure
there's no one who wouldn't go down on death (*your
blueeyed boy*), forget to come up
for air: I have been half in love
myself. He's dead by now, found them
at the Grand Avenue Mall, the unfashionable
Club 219, where white men sometimes go
to pick up hot black numbers (never mine).
Couldn't you just eat him up right there? Come
here. Eleven skulls, one skeleton, a freezer
stocked with body parts. They found bones
in the basement they still can't identify.
Identified with him. I found myself.

Every white man on my bus home looks
like him, what I'd want to be destroyed
by, want to be. (I thought I would

abase myself for love or any damage:
I was wrong.) The man next to me
wouldn't touch me, moved away
when I sat down. One day I'll wash my hands
of this, a waste of all that circumstance, waste of
my good time. His more than one hundred pages
of confession note "my consuming lust to experience
their bodies." Every white man
I can see. What's it like not to want? It's late
May in Milwaukee, thirty degrees at night.

2

A man naked in bed beside you has a smell
that's quite particular, not unpleasant but
distinct. It stays in the room all morning
after he's gone, you don't know where
it comes from. You'd like to know
what's in his head, or what he had
for lunch. Asleep, the body lying
next to you seems just so much
red meat, some matter muttering
to itself. Dead bodies have a smell also
which some men will do anything
to understand. Who wouldn't want
to feel what he has felt, these
clumsy hands on every interior
of him? Not I, but sometimes
always *me*, small case

against. "Mass murderers are men
who can't control their interest
in other people." They're men consumed
by curiosity. Close enough to get inside
his skin, to take his smell and make it
mine. They couldn't get the smell
out of the building; I can't get this
out of me. An experiment
in how to become someone else
who isn't moving anymore.

Apollo on What the Boy Gave

Eyes the color of winter water,
eyes the winter of water where I

Quoits in the Spartan month
Hyacinthius, the game
joins us, pronounces
us god and boy: I toss him
the discus thinking *This is mine*
and wind says *Not yet*

Memory with small hairs
pasted to pale wet skin
(the flower *hyacinthos*,
perhaps a fritillaria, not
the modern *Hyacinthus orientalis*)

After he smells of orange groves,
spreads white ass meat for me
him with a hole drilled in him I keep trying
to fill: I ease my way into his orchard

(the ornamental Liliaceae
genera, including the spring
-flowering *Crocus* and *Hyacinthus*,
and the summer-flowering
Hemerocallis or day lily: also
Amaryllis, Hippeastrum, and *Narcissus*)

A blow struck by jealous Zephyrus, or
Boreas, by other accounts:
his skin annotated by the wound
that explicates his mortality
in red pencil, wind edits him down to
withering perennial, shriveled bulb

(perhaps a pre-Hellenic god, his
precise relationship to Apollo
still obscure, though clearly
a subordinate)

Him with a hole I keep trying
to make, dead meat of white
blooms in hand

(onion as well, garlic, leek,
chive, and asparagus)

And where he was
this leafless stalk (bluebell,
tulip, torch lily, trillium:
snowdrop, Solomon's
seal) I break to take for my own,
black at the core of blossoming

(a bell shaped nodding flower,
usually solitary)

Apollo Steps in Daphne's Footprints

Everywhere one turns
a god, someone turning into one
(cedar, cypress, sandalwood
camphor tree, cinnamon, juniper)
green as new time ripening
on the vine, hunting shoots
down into bloom, relays
and intermittencies

I made her, break her down
to twig stripped clean, a girl
-shaped slip of driftwood, mandrake
root that makes a fatal sound

She's made of some aromatic wood
(common myrtle, eucalyptus) and
I'm running after trees, tripping
over brambles, creepers and fragrant
underbrush, magnolia or japonica
(sperm smell over everything). One branch
just out of reach, sweet smelling leaves
some kindling, good for burning through
October to the season's
other side, smoke for the bees

Tracking the scent of lack
through rills and branches, freshets
streaming over pebbles (scent of
no, not at all, overpowering

odor of negation), I lost the trail
(she's moving further
into verblessness, the roots
of meaning: true aloe, not
these bracts of sassafras
and cassia: bees swathe
her in hum, leave the honey
behind, beetles pollinate her)

and ran into a tree (I am
the hunted?), stayed there
centuries (fox to the wolves
that tear summer in half?)
a light seen through
dense crowns: *Laurus nobilis*
sweet bay, bay laurel, noon's
lush lingua, sexual lexicon

A pocketful of fame in the hand
crushed leaves staining the air
I place this chaplet on my brow
(a crown of wintergreen)
and I am the sun

Semantics at Four P.M.

He smiles, says *What's happening?*
and I say somewhere
someone's setting electrodes to someone's testicles
who's been immersed two hours in ice water

up to his shoulders, he can't remember
what day it used to be. Somewhere someone
is being disemboweled with a
serrated blade, fish-knife

to slit open two fresh trout
he had for dinner last
week, Wednesday celebration
sizzling in its battered aluminum pan

over an open campfire
in a clearing, gleaming
pan and fish and fire and the water
that put out the fire, and

he looks down at his intestines, small
and large uncoiling, spoiling
by the unpaved road, surprised
the slick should glisten so, even

at noon, this close
to the equator, is it still summer
there, I never can remember
seasons. Several things are

happening, someone is being kicked repeatedly
in the ribs by three cops (he's black, blue
by now too, purple boot
marks, bruise treads), someone else

keeps falling against the wet cement floor
of his holding cell, he can't stop
falling, somebody
stop him, then he does, stopped watch, old

-fashioned, with a broken
spring coil mechanism, and someone
could find it facedown on the sidewalk, hold it
up to the light, say *I can fix this,*

but doesn't. Somewhere four teenaged boys
are playing hackeysack by a stream bed
on the verge of story, one
has an erection he wants

to go down, and someone thinks about
dinner, someone says *Sure looks like rain.*

Cygnus

For Geoffrey Nutter

Persons reminded me of birds, a boy
who is a swan and is not mine,
white feathers that go by
clouds. He figures as constellation, clouds
in tight formation, forming him
or his impossibility of skin. That he is seen
to be beautiful, that he is called by strangers'
names, almost persuaded of September: that he
is torn from the white he makes
his home, falling as snow, down.
Boy who became a swan, buoyed through
blank night, stick figure fixed to several skies: wing
for a writing arm, he is a poet
scribbling down stars, their mouths
pinned open, hungering
in place. That he is seen to take flight
in magnitudes, that he persuades
himself to be observed at different proximities
to the horizon, that light bends
for him relative to the position he takes
regarding the sun. Star-mouth,
cloud-lip, northerly wing, my hands
are talced with a dust of feathers,
my hands are full of birds, all thumbs.
You fly through me.

Weather Comes from the West

He's all states and princes, colonies
and continental drift, waging
plate tectonics on his way to rain:
territories of avowal and random

vowels. Clouds are interruptions
in the blue, occlusions pregnant
with rain or other inclemencies,
unkind transitions filled

with gods (my enemy muse).
Also this is the sea. Someone
looked in on color and found it lacking
something green: all treason,

heretic to froth and spume, and
the ones who stayed with nothing
inside. Night is a wire hung with
small sounds, philosophy of wolves

in eclipse, or any disposition
towards blackened white.
Sibling forest, brother
town: tides in the air, tides in

the earth, miles of lines downed
and by unlikely conditions diagnosed.

Manifest

Sir star, Herr Lenz, white season body
master snapping masts in half, absent
winds' workmanship: what window
will I look you through, what brook, stream

creaking past fretwork weeds, clouds
in the context of cold? Lord knot
to be untied, skiff hard alee ill winds:
a hiss of wish and cinders and I

am warm, crossing dazed oceans by hand
to sow the doubtful sea with drought. Mine
of rain and seize and sluice, you change

your mind again, a rage for green waves'
open vowels, undrinkable. No talking
to the weeds, no talking with the snow.

Imaginary Elegy

The manifest scatters likeness
like white light, gods
cut through my body like a sword
in the hands of a dead hero, he who
accomplishes, whittles
me down into perfection, or if
I won't, then less than that,
an absence at the edges
of narration, mention me. Love
burns like incense in gold censers
and cannot forgive (empire
of essential oils annexing air),
who can withstand
being loved for long.

When light pours out of me
(like love, resembling, resembling),
citronella oil and myrrh, white
peppermint, less hardy
and more prized, like blood
whose savor is sweet
in the nostrils of gods
when it steams on
uncovered altars, streams from
the fresh-cut throat. I would
be beautiful, burnt wilderness
at bay, and what would that
be like? Siege of light glints, nicks
marred skin. Elektra always forgets

Iphigeneia, bitch sister
sharpening the blades, the finest silver.

FATA MORGANA

Orpheus Plays the Bronx

When I was ten (*no, younger*
than that), my mother tried
to kill herself (*without the facts*
there can't be faith). One death
or another every day, Tanqueray bottles
halo the bed and she won't wake up
all weekend. In the myth book's color
illustration, the poet turns around
inside the mouth of hell to look at her
losing him (*because it's not her fault*
they had to meet there): so he can keep her
somewhere safe, save her place
till she comes back. Some say
she stepped on an asp, a handful of pills
littered the floor with their blues,
their red and yellow music. Al Green
was on the radio. (*You were*
at school, who's ever even seen
an asp?) It bruised her heel
purple and black. So death
could get some color to fill out
his skin, another bony white boy
jealous of her laugh too loud, her
That's my song when Barry White
comes on. He's just got
to steal it, he can't resist
a bad pun, never never gonna give her
up, or back. The pictures don't prove
anything, but one thing I remember

about the myth's still true:
the man can't live if she does.
She survived to die for good.

How People Disappear

If this world were mine, the stereo
starts, but can't begin
to finish the phrase. I might survive
it, someone could add, but that
someone's not here. She's crowned
with laurel leaves, the place
where laurel leaves would be
if there were leaves, she's not
medieval Florence, not
Blanche of Castile. Late March
keeps marching in old weather,
another slick of snow to trip
and fall into, another bank
of inconvenient fact. The sky
is made of paper and white reigns,
shredded paper pools into her afterlife,
insurance claims and hospital reports,
bills stamped "Deceased," sign here
and here, a blank space where she
would have been. My sister
said *We'll have to find another*
Mommy.
            And this is how
loss looks, my life in black plastic
garbage bags, a blue polyester suit
a size too small. Mud music
as they packed her in
damp ground, it's always raining
somewhere, in New Jersey,

while everyone was thinking about
fried chicken and potato salad,
caramel cake and lemonade.
Isn't that a pretty dress
they put her in? She looks so
lifelike. (Tammi Terrell
collapsed in Marvin Gaye's arms
onstage. For two hundred points,
what was the song?) Trampled
beneath the procession, her music.

Pieces of sleep like pieces of shale
crumble through my four A.M.
(a flutter of gray that could be
rain), unable to read this thing
that calls itself the present.
She's lost among the spaces
inside letters, moth light, moth wind,
a crumpled poem in place of love.

For My Mother in Lieu of Mourning

It takes a thing so long to be true. I don't want
my dead back, not any more, dreaming they're just
in hiding. The body stiffens into *I'm awake*, chilled
by a window left open all night. Dust grays

the screen, truncates the run-down view
of strip mall loading dock and idling delivery
truck fumes: unseasonable cold, no birds, everything
gets dirty fast. Then memory becomes rain

after days of overcast, wet panes blur into blind
clouds learning to let go. Too accurate a memory
is the cure for dreams. Your body of brackish water,
black, opaque, impossible to see through

to the bottom, swim across to shore:
I've been drowning in my sleep
too long, when will I stop comparing you? Today
my hands discover distance, the heart I imagined

I had: this lying signifier settled from time to time
by ghosts. The words return in single file, repeat
themselves: cold and uninhabited, my heart's
healed over under ice. Would you have frozen

in these lines? You were their possibility:
now love must find another shape. You left me here
with what you saved me from, and I am equal
to that: absence, wind tangled in a winter tree,

defeat dangling from stripped branches,
or perhaps it's just a plastic grocery bag.

Pear Tree, Bartlett, Quotations

Unswim the sky, clouds row across
and sink, it's we who drown. Ballast
overboard, it's me I'm scared of (song
said that), July hangs white
on heat looms. My mother, my
humiliation, born under the archer's
sign, under the broken arrows,
snapped string and shattered bow.
(See, I have winged you, wordless
woman, "him" doesn't happen
here. Watch over me as I
slip underneath, unlight
my eyes.) Shadows scrawl across slate
paving stones, the bitten fruit
falls bitter to the lawn. Squirrels
spit it out. The green
fruit ripens on the ground, yellows
toward rot and chewed-through browns.
Later I'm walking toward despair
with the other roadside detritus,
some fatal and irrevocable countryside
southwest of who I am.
Green leafy inedible words
(*for ornamental use only* sign says,
song says too) give shade to roadkill,
possums, rabbits, and raccoons,
black men who don't know better
than to wander a county highway
all night, fucked by the gods

and left for dead on the dislocated
shoulder of Route 96B. Archer's wandered
out of sight, cloudcover quarter-moon
changes every yes to no.
The laden branch can't be picked,
all that unripe just in reach.

At Weep

Can't move can't speak can't think to wonder
why that's so. Song says *I still
believe*, can't think of what, who
that might be. Their faces gather

blackness, can't be seen. Song says *I*
and *I* and *I*. It sounds like *cry*,
like someone crying in the woods
by Stewart Park (the dirty woods, let me

be filthy, stain me, let the bones
come together, bone
to its bone and tainted too):
like someone crying but he has

no eyes no ears no mouth no
voice to speak of. Speak to me.
Can't hear you anymore, can't ask
for more. Song keeps repeating

*shit where you eat, don't shit
where you eat.* The day
begins with burning, then remembers
to wake up: sweetbitter resins,

pollens, dripping cum smells
flower, white. Highway's haunted
by remembered men and boys, no light
but passing pickup trucks, Nero burning

in the Tiber's unmade bed:
ecology of lack and want
and never lack of want, no never
want. Want to go home. Not yet

a *you*, or *he*, an *it* (no want
of want), a something to be seen
and see what comes
of it (can't see anything now, walking
past black woods). Here he comes.
Song litters upstate New York maps
with classical towns, Attica, Utica, Syracuse,
Troy, lining the throughways with Latin
and Greek: Ithaca and the other islands
fingering slim lakes. Seneca
slits his wrists in the bath,
too late for life in ancient Rome.

Things Waiting to Be Dangerous

Something gets tired of being said,
I left my love of me behind
to fester in the slough of cast-off self

-regard with other toxic wastes, condoms
I forgot and umbrellas that don't
close, festering piles of newsprint, misplaced

phone numbers, things I never understood
how to use: new shoes I wore holes into the soles of
walking home in the rain and the soaked

stained socks, paper bags of burned-out light bulbs
and clear bandages, pill boxes, urine
samples, nail clippings and used razor

blades, danger biohazard; flotation
devices in case of water landing, plastic
bags of saline solution, things

I never knew I had. (Bring it on, the waiting
in a basement stall for someone to sit down,
tap one foot *yes*, the workmen's overtime

contempt, a waste of spirit and I don't even
drink. Bring all the men in bedrooms
bathrooms backrooms bookstores alleys

who left me unsatisfied, came with me
after all. I miss them now. Bring on my
retrovirus, invisible catastrophe, distracted

palindrome and abstract doom,
another decade's style in sex, or maybe
it was imported, bring me something to drink. Something

gets tired, undresses for bed.) I've considered you
these things I never should have
thrown away, said I was drowning,

but it was never as good
as when you took me down, went under.
I'd ask the god of the good green sea

for a waterfall's rush into brink, sputter
and jangle of brined plunge, but I don't
know his name. (Fill my mouth with water,

salt, with sperm, and wash away
the words.) Whitewater emptinesses
hurl me into themselves, a place

gets tired, gets read too many times:
dawn-burnished lake undrinkable,
raw sewage and dead seaweed, russet

and gold toxins greet the day. Rot
smell lingers all week, I'd love to
go down again.

Eve's Awakening

I woke and was alone in some new world—
there wasn't world before, or wasn't me
to see it, call it world. Birds made as if to speak

to someone I couldn't see, trees waved green arms
like flags swimming light winds, echoing clouds
that ornamented blue. Everything

echoed there, held conversation
with itself, or with some likeness
of itself. I was alone, and woke

into the sound of world: rose
into that colloquy of purple and yellow flowers
I couldn't name. I heard some waters

calling me, rose and walked
toward that music, and lay down beside a sky
that had laid itself down for me, the sky laid low

with waiting for me, having given up
above. My face waited for me
in the singing water, welcomed me

with my own gaze, my own lips
rose up to kiss my name
into my voice. But then another voice

called me away from me, calling my face
his likeness, and made me
half, who had been whole, beside myself

lying there beside the lake of sky.
He called me by a name I'd never heard,
tried to enclose my hand in his: that garden

suddenly seemed small, enclosed
on every side by God, something that said
to call him that. Everything sang me

but him, I heard a voice and turned away.

Objects in Mirror Are Closer than They Appear

World Trade Center, September 11, 2001

I stow this moment with all the other baggage
too heavy to be carried or left
behind. Roadside church sign says *The Lord*
is the Lord who made us the way we are us.
He scatters the remnants and collects
them at a later date (unspecified): sorts them
into neat piles. I have watched twin towers fall
a dozen times. An absence moves through
the wreckage while the light stays put; the rats
will have to find another home.

Song keeps repeating *I watched you suffer*
even after the song's turned off.

History picks her way in high heels
through the structural redundancy (still shimmering
with its recentness, its haze of airborne ash
and grit), compassion makes his way through the structured
inequality in blue serge suit to interview survivors of
the structural adjustment, the combined
and uneven development that bursts into flames
at half an hour intervals, implodes
in slow motion with a televisual sigh
(catches up with photogenic falling bodies).

Song wants to soothe the sidewalk misery
into grief, smooth the debris into a shroud.

Lamed truth hobbles into another dark
through crumpled girders and concrete, calibrating
ruin and song, ruining the song
for the sake of what was life: hands out these
glass splinters, mercies and atrocities
that can't be lulled into music,
the ignorance we call innocence.
They taste like burning (a violent antidote),
incapable of caring if it harmonizes, or
unwilling to succumb again.

Song won't shut up, keeps saying *Don't look
down.* Justice tries to listen for a low tapping sound.

Self-Portrait in the New World Order

You're walking down the street alone,
absorbed in the anticipation of a lunchtime salad
with that crusty olive bread you like so much,
and suddenly you're marching in formation
in a crowd, it's called a regiment.
You seem to be a soldier this time, you learn
to be at war. You're never really in danger
because you know you can't die
in your dreams, but sometimes
you wonder who told you that and whether
they could be trusted. The sidewalk is split
and uneven because of the shrapnel
and the artillery shells; yesterday
you didn't know the definition of artillery,
but today you know how to use it, all kinds
of field ordnance. "Ordnance" is a word
you'd never heard before. Every time
there's so much to notice, so much
to remember and write down. Here's
a little notebook with rubbed-down corners
for your back pocket. It's the little things
that distinguish one war from another,
tonight your shoes are black standard issue
marching boots that lace halfway up
your calves, whereas the other night
you had no shoes, or the shoes you'd lost
were beige bedroom slippers whose plush
offered no protection from the slush and rain
you trudged through. The subway crash

distracted you from that, now
you're climbing over the wreckage
to the next sheltered position, air thick
with morning mist (you're shivering), smoke
and a haze of acrid dust, it burns your lungs.
You're clambering through accordioned
cars, where are those twisted rails
that won't carry any passengers taking you?

A Handful of Sand

I'm always putting things in poems
where I think they'll keep, lying
to the lying gods to make a way
out of whatever ways I have.
The rooms we wander through
on a day of no significance
are white, are beige, are gray, nothing
of any importance will happen
today. A fake fragment of Greek frieze
frames three plaster women in pleated chitons
sitting on a bus, or so it looks
from here, a krater holds a plastic plant
(saw palmetto, perhaps) that's following
them, but they don't seem to be
moved. Graffiti on the men's room stall
reads "TEXT," reads "SIGN,"
and also the word "DEUCE"
scratched into green-painted metal.

Think of all the blunder and fault
in the world, a noisy lexicon
of mistake, hoots, jargles, squawks,
and rasps, think of all the bending
and the breaking of oak boughs.
Think of the quartz beach wrecked
by recent hurricanes, driftwood
and seaweed beginning to stink,
plastic cup lids I mistook for shells.

(We have seen the wind
by what it leaves behind, its wreckage
and detritus, but the water
won't be wounded.)

File this pearl-smooth conch interior
under *no*, press it against your ear
as if it were the spirit radio,
and you were walking down the street
tuned to just one voice, wading
waist-high through shallow light.
The minutes continue their shine, the shapes
of color change and turn; a wind
blows through my skin
and you renew the weather.
I will not entirely die.

With the Wind Blowing Through It

Special instructions
to the spinner of webs, the knotter
of strings, the weaver
of cloth, the plaiter of nets,
the thrower of ropes
over chasms, special instructions
to the builder of bridges,
the stitcher of wounds and torn skin,
the cable and the thread:

Special instructions to the rain
and assorted precipitations,
evaporations, condensations
connecting earth and air, one place
melting into the brother place
just for a moment, my place
and how I lost it:

Special instructions
to the layers of roads, the asphalt,
blacktop, and cracked macadam, special
instructions to the puddled
ends of slanted driveways, muddled water
pooling its resources, reflecting
on the live oaks, longleaf
pines, the skies trees stitch together
while clouds disperse, air crowded
with plant sex, my nostrils
filled with plant sperm:

The same sky keeps happening
but differently each time
(today with finches in it)

Light Years

A god can't do it, wants to touch all that
mortality, but his hands slip through
it, his fingers have no prints, no
grip. He's too symmetrical, has been too
perfected to fit himself into the zigs
and zags, warped planes and random
crevices, snags and tangles, cracks
and wrong notes and dropped
stitches. *Too true*, wind whispers, it sighs
right through him: the world all Daphne
and him no kind of tree.

What's underneath things or inside
them, cranks and cams and hammers, flywheels
and toothed gears, whirs and clicks and grindings
down, ticking out their working through
of function, motion, form: you find them
even microscopic, or too big
to see unaided: expose the seams and joints
for inspection, clear as never
and never so close. You break open days
to show what they're made of, all flesh
is sunlight, a machine
plugged into a main sequence yellow dwarf
star. Late afternoon flatters my skin
with pattern, and then the setting sun undoes
the picture. Dark, light, bright
slip through my fingers, color distinctions
fade with the day.

You walk ahead as if you know
the way, full of purpose and intent
on seeing what's to be seen
if you look hard enough, look deep
enough, so certain the world is as you find it.
(A pileated woodpecker taps on a dead
scrub pine, I can't find it even when you
point it out.) I hang back with the noncommittal
wind (the sound of wind), wandering away
from glory. You call me back
to the world of things, sometimes
I don't know why I should go there.

RED CLAY WEATHER

Attempted Birdcage Number Three

The visual surround collapsed into
pine tree, main power line, mailbox, garbage
can pulled up beside the road, repeating
blues and greens; the little interruptions

got bigger and bigger, building gaps
among the live oak branches. For days
the mower wouldn't start
because of cold, finally cut the damp yard

down to size. Grass mocked our aspirations to be good
with its tangled root systems, its determination
not to be supplanted; dew shone in early sunlight
like virtue and evaporated. Facts are like frames:

we mapped the plants and called them
weather, mapped the plants
and called them soil, sandy loam
rain drains right through

down to the water table, down
to Boulder Creek, to Thompson Bayou, ends up
in Escambia Bay, undrinkable. Squirrels harass
the birdfeeders and won't scare, the finches

stay away. The garden's overgrown
with weeds' strength of will, done in
by an early frost, leaves wilt and wither
under the naked-air agenda. My body

is so porous, let this weather disappear me.

To Be Free

It's winter in my body all year long, I wake up
with music pouring from my skin, morning
burning behind closed blinds. Dead
light, dead warmth on dead skin

cells, the sky is wrong
again. Hope clings to me like damp
sheets, lies to my skin. As if I were a coat
wearing my bare body out on loan,

accumulated layers of mistake
and identity, never mine.
I'm dressed as so many people, well known
wrong me reviving my old heresies,

praying them into sunset
and the weather they'll become:
folding them into snow. The forecasts
are always accurate, the only promises

kept. Foolish Narcissus frittered himself away
to a flower, Echo suffered down her life
to someone else's syllables wind throws
away. Neither knew how to survive

the period style, long days
in their disastrous completeness.
I won't let the myths outlive me, won't drown
in my nostalgia for the here and now.

I lie down in imperial purple
as if I were the sun, lay my body down
in distance. Correct all deviations
and make the moon change its tune.

The New Life

I woke in the middle of a wooded
trailer park (in the middle
of somebody's lies), lying mired in a muddle
about where I was, with nothing
I could call my own: no shoes, no shirt, no pants,

no socks, no job or occupation, income
none. Wrecked mobile homes
on either side hinted at ruin
come and gone astray, what might return
for dinner, bringing friends

and friends of friends. The earth dressed down
in withered grasses and crashed trees, pine straw
and rusted household appliances,
made a welcome for me, made a grave
to mock me back to sleep. Raw sunlight

ignited my dissolving bones,
buried me alive in my disintegrating
body. How long it takes not to move.
My tarnished-penny idioms discoloring
unfinished loam, knife-edged

and neverward, I decided
not to die that day, made my mobility
my theme: stood up to red clay dust
and downed corrugated fencing, uncollected
with the other storm debris.

My Mother Was No White Dove

no dove at all, coo-rooing through the dusk
and foraging for small seeds
My mother was the clouded-over night
a moon swims through, the dark against which stars
switch themselves on, so many already dead
by now (stars switch themselves off
and are my mother, she was never
so celestial, so clearly seen)

My mother was the murderous flight of crows
stilled, black plumage gleaming
among black branches, taken
for nocturnal leaves, the difference
between two darks:

a cacophony of needs
in the bare tree silhouette,
a flight of feathers, scattering
black. She was the night
streetlights oppose (perch
for the crows, their purchase on sight),
obscure bruise across the sky
making up names for rain

My mother always falling
was never snow, no kind
of bird, pigeon or crow

What Nature Doesn't Show

It's always raining in my dreams,
I'm always lacking something
that I need, an umbrella, shoes, my peace
of mind, or just the right direction
home, another piece of my mind
I'll never find, far from what I'd want
to be. I carry these things
far into the night, or one just like
it, whitening into dawn
while rain wipes away the wax-paper
moon, the damp overgrown yard
moves into meadowhood, another
lush polluted pastoral. The wind
is simplified in such weather, wet windows
hold memory at a distance, drowning
liquid stars: a loss too far away
to reach the human world, barely touched
by the finger of fact. The body
is a body of water too, rain makes of me
a lake or pool or puddle, any fluid gathering
expanding and contracting
to the rhythm of imaginary tides'
forgotten or misplaced intentions.
I wonder, who invented water?

My Mother Dated Otis Redding

My mother is laughing in the hallway with her friends
I don't like much, maybe the numbers runner
who gives me dollars to go see movies
while they fuck, a mattress propped in the doorway
where there's no door. I know what's "fuck," and "dick,"
and "pussy." They're "tipsy," she says, they're having
a good time. "Don't I deserve a good time
now and then?" I'm looking through the telescope
I just got from a catalogue, while they
break out the Tanqueray; I don't know what
that is. They're putting on some records, it's
1970, Nixon's president; there's a dock in one song
and I don't know how to whistle, but I know
what's a dock, and a bay. There aren't many stars
because of the streetlights, it's the Bronx,
the singer sounds sad, he's dead. My mother
says, "You know, I went to high school
with him, back in Macon," and everybody says
"I'll bet," and she laughs. I wish I was his
son, I wish they'd all go home. It's late and I just want
to go to bed, but she just wants to have a good
time. I turn my telescope on the Puerto Rican couple
fighting, kissing in a window across the concrete
courtyard, three parrots escaped from the loading
dock freezing in a trash tree, it's
November, neighborhood kids throwing rocks
at each other from bicycles, my mother standing in the hallway
with a paper cup of Tanqueray, or lying
in the hallway in a pool of her own shit.

Flying

You think continually of those you truly hate, it keeps you
up at night, even with the fan you run to block out the badneighborhood
noises, the feet walking by that might pause at your
apartment door. There are too many people to list, but you try
anyway: the kid sitting on the table behind you who kicked you
in the back all through social studies class and when you got up
and shoved him the teacher kicked you out into the hall; the kid
who threw crayons at you in art class while singing an obscene
song about your mother until you put him in a headlock (you were
thrown out then too, to think about what you'd done); the kid
taking karate who kicked you in the stomach because he thought
you'd stolen his seat, though really it was yours. There's always so
much kicking, in and out. The kids in your neighborhood who
threw rocks at you or tried to steal your bus pass on the way to
school, the kids at school who sat on your stomach during recess
and banged your egghead against the playground asphalt, the Italian
kids three blocks up Crotona who threw a vegetable crate on your
head while calling out "Hey chocolate milk!" one afternoon on your
way home from school. There are always so many kids. Sometimes
you think you hate too much, but there's so much to hate, so many
people have done you wrong, now that you think about it maybe
you don't hate enough. Your stepfather who attacked your mother
with a butcher knife, was that before or after the restraining order,
who cut all the wires inside the new tape deck she bought you ("I'm
going to make it like a vegetable") because he thought she spoiled
you, and she did. But you weren't his son and it wasn't his money.
He shut off the electricity to your room one afternoon to make you
wash the drawings from the walls. When you become emperor of
the universe they'll all be punished, everyone who was ever cruel to

you will pay. It's not enough to have them tortured, because they'll die and then their pain will end. You'll use nerve induction, maybe that's not the right phrase, whatever they call it when you stimulate the pain centers directly and there's no physical damage, so they can suffer over and over. You'll have every one of them brought before you on your jeweled throne on its raised dais and you'll smile kindly as you explain to them their crimes and especially their punishment, they'll be dragged away pleading for mercy you won't have, and finally you'll be able to sleep.

Falling

For Bradford Morrow

You share a bed with your mother in the two-room tenement walkup, because you're afraid to sleep on the living room sofa on account of the rats. You don't wet the bed anymore. One evening you were sitting on her lap, maybe she was reading you a story, you always hated being read to, when a huge one ran right past the chair, you thought it was a big dust ball or some kind of indoor tumbleweed. "What's that, Mommy?" you asked, and she answered, "That's a rat." There were more rats than people in that apartment building, or so your mother said. When you wake up to go to the bathroom in the middle of the night you put on a pair of her high heels and bang a broom on the splintering wood floor to scare the rats away or at least warn them to get out of your way. You've counted the number of steps to the bathroom, counted the number of steps to the kitchen. They say parents shouldn't let a child have anything to drink too close to bedtime or he'll be getting up all night, but you've only got your mother. One night you wake up and there's a vampire standing in the doorway without a door to close off the bedroom from the living room. You know that he's a vampire because his skin glows blue-white like the fluorescent kitchen lights (his hair is a pure white crew cut, glowing too) and he's sleek in a black suit and staring at you with his dead white eyes. You duck your head under the covers and when you've mustered up the courage to peek out again he's disappeared. Your mother doesn't believe you when you tell her about him and it makes you mad at her. Another night you look out the bars over the bedroom window and there's a dinosaur staring in across the fire escape it could rip away with just one tug, a *Tyrannosaurus rex* with carnivorous intent studying the puny mammals huddled inside their den, but even that deep in the dark you suspect you might have conjured it up from watching too many *Creature Feature* movies on Channel 9 when you get home from school. There's a new one every afternoon and you try to catch them all. Even when you watch something scary well before dark, you have nightmares later on, but you watch anyway. You close your eyes and it's gone, stays gone when you open them again. When you move into the brand-new housing project, you have your own room and your own twin bed with Mickey Mouse sheets you got at Disney World, and there are no rats. You don't have a twin, it takes you a while to get used to sleeping by yourself, you feel alone and vulnerable to all the things that wake up when you go to sleep. They don't have names and they don't have shapes, but if you leave the closet door open before you go to bed they can collect in that dark, and you can't get up and close it once you've turned out the light. If you keep your whole body under the sheet nothing can hurt you, not even when you feel yourself falling, plummeting into a void that isn't sleep, and you hear voices laughing and muttering and calling to each other. Your grandmother in Georgia says that's when a witch is riding you, but she's a senile old woman who wets herself sometimes and wears her gray wigs crooked. She thinks the pennies she doles out like little candies (not often enough) can actually buy anything these days. Where would a witch ride you to? As long as no part sticks out from under the sheet you're safe, even when you wake up paralyzed, unable to move and always in the most vulnerable posture, you can't gather your voice to cry for help and some mornings you can't even breathe, you don't know for how long except that it's too long. Sometimes it's just a game, you lie there perfectly still though you could change position if you wanted to, tap your left foot or wag three fingers of your right hand, you want to see how long you can refuse to move, now it's in your control.

Some Dreams He Forgot

Dreams in which I realize that I'm not wearing shoes; I'm walking through fields of broken glass or sidewalks of rain, slush, snow with naked feet, stepping carefully so as not to cut myself. My feet get dirty fast, pebbles and dead leaves cling to them. Dreams in which I'm wearing only one shoe. Dreams in which I realize I've forgotten my shoes five minutes before my flight and have to go back for them, but I never make it anywhere near home; the airport becomes a labyrinth and I never find my way out of the maze.

Dreams in which I'm not wearing pants, running my errands obliviously. Sometimes people look askance, but no one ever says anything. It must be a minor faux-pas, like passing gas in an elevator or not saying "Excuse me" when you brush past someone. I'm browsing in the local independent bookstore, looking through modern poetry and Adorno, when I realize that I've driven all the way downtown, walked blocks from my car to the store, wearing nothing but a T-shirt; I'm naked from the waist down. The store owner lends me a pair of shorts, but I'm not sure if they will fit.

Dreams in which I'm trying to go somewhere that should be just around the corner, just a block ahead, but the way gets more and more convoluted. I'm running through a maze of muddy streets (sometimes without my shoes), passing Marilyn Manson talking on a cell phone and being passed by a muscular runner with a shaved head who thinks I'm racing with him, but no matter how fast I run I never arrive. I'm supposed to look at an apartment and I've forgotten the address, even forgotten the last name of the man I'm meant to meet, but it doesn't matter because I'll never find my way.

Dreams in which I'm taking the subway home, a trip I've made a dozen times, but I end up somewhere I've never been, some barely populated wasteland from which I have to find my way back. It's the end of the line, or just the wrong stop. Dreams in which the elevated train derails miles from where I meant to go; I barely survive the crash and have to walk home bewildered through an urban wilderness.

Dreams in which I can hardly walk, my legs are so heavy and weak, as if they were made of cement or lead. I'm trying to run across a field from danger, zombies or perhaps there's a war on, but I can hardly move, and the danger's catching up fast. If it hasn't seen me, it will soon.

Dreams in which I should be able to fly but can barely stay aloft, and that only by intense concentration, my feet dragging against the crowns of trees, protruding rocks and elevated patches of ground, or barely clearing the flat roofs of low buildings. Sometimes from outside it looks like soaring, I've escaped whatever trap or monster threatened me, but I always feel that I'm about to sink.

Dreams in which I should be able to breathe water but instead I drown (only one of these, actually, in which I'm saved from drowning by a talking whale).

Why am I always dreaming about not getting what I need?

✳

Dreams in which I wake up to the sound of someone trying to force the locked bedroom door. I hear the knob clicking and turning, but I can't move, can't cry out "Who is it?" or "Go away" or "Help," or even open my eyes. Then I shudder awake to a familiar rhythmic hum, it's just the fan I run all night to block out noises and help me sleep. Betrayed by sound again.

Dreams in which the doors won't lock or even close properly, the door suddenly shrinks so it's smaller than the frame, the deadbolt becomes a simple hook, and something dangerous is coming, a zombie, werewolf, vampire, or just a deathless serial killer. Sometimes it's something doors won't keep out anyway, some shapeless nameless evil—the featureless is always frightening.

Dreams in which an unstoppable werewolf is coming for the young; he'll kill everyone in the house if we're not turned over. Before anyone can stop me I scoop up all the young (including my Robert) and put them in my pocket—I have a shrinking ray—and then I seal us all up in the panic room, totally selfenclosed and impenetrable, with its own supplies of food and air. We'll wait the werewolf out, and ignore everyone else's screams.

Dreams in which I start seeing hard, unfamiliar faces at the porthole windows of the doors at my private high school, furtive men in black trench coats, black hats, and high black leather boots. My friends start disappearing one by one, and the white students start acting strangely toward us black students, distant and cold. Then we're invited on a field trip, just the black kids, a special opportunity they say. As we're walking to the bus I see a giant hose leading to it and I know they're planning to gas us. I run, but am trapped in a cement stairwell. A black janitor tells the commandant where I'm hiding (*You fool*, I think, *they'll kill you too when you're no use to them*, but the commandant just laughs: there's no need to pursue me because the doors form an airtight seal; I'll slowly suffocate. I sit on the concrete stairs with my head in my hands and wake to the sound of his laughter echoing against the whitewashed cinderblock walls.

Dreams in which all the white people have gone away, and I'm one of the leaders of this new world, where everyone's free. Then the white men come back from outer space, we welcome them to the world we've made, but they just say "We've come to take our planet back." They conquer us, execute many, imprison many more, and suddenly we're all slaves, when yesterday the world was ours. I'm someone's butler or valet, I'm walking down the corridors of headquarters on an errand and I have to pee; I go into an executive men's room, which is strictly off-limits, whites only, but I can't hold it until the colored men's room. A white executive is in there, an important man, and demands to know just what I think I'm doing, "Boy, where do you think you are?" I've had enough. I smash his face into the urinal repeatedly, gouge out his eye with the flush handle, and then I'm running with blood on my shirt, hiding in the crawlspaces and climbing through the ventilation pipes. I pass rooms full of white people who could have been my friends, hear them talk and laugh like human beings, but I know that they'll betray me if they can.

Dreams in which I'm in a burning building (how did I get there?) with Seth Green and three other young guys (ten years from now that name will mean nothing), and we're running down the stairs to get outside before the flames consume us. We reach a huge window two or three stories tall and they all jump out through the glass into the pouring rain, but I look and think that there's no way I'd make that jump, so I walk out through the door, where it's not raining anymore. We sit on the grass (it's night by now) and watch the building collapse, and one of the young men explains that they're on a tour of Moravian churches—there are only three in the entire country. I say, "But there's one right there," and dreaming ends.

Dreams in which I'm in a bathroom where every man or boy is having sex but me, dreams in which I'm looking for the cruisy bathroom or bookstore where men have sex with men without talking, just down the street or across campus, just up a set of stairs in the dorm or library or classroom building that never end. The promised sex keeps getting farther away, I keep being waylaid by conversations or suspicious eyes, or I'm just walking, walking, searching until I wake up. Too many dreams in which I never get to sex.

Dreams in which I'm in the shower and suddenly realize that I should have been teaching a class for the past half a semester, I rush to the Greyhound station and by the time I get to campus it's evening, and I don't even know where the class should be meeting. Dreams in which I've forgotten to take a high school class and I have to go back for a semester. The building is a maze and I don't even know what room I'm supposed to be in; I end up in the wrong class over and over without even a notebook or a pen, or I'm wandering the halls all day until the bell rings for the end of classes. Dreams in which I have to go back to my isolated little college in Vermont to take one last class; I have two master's degrees but that doesn't matter, and I'm waiting in line for my room key again.

Dreams in which I have to return to college and I can't find my room. The dorm turns into a maze in which I'm trapped, I keep passing the same rooms over and over, never mine, the same living room and kitchen, I go up and down the endless stairs and all I want to do is lie down in the bed I've never seen, all my belongings are already in the room and they'll never be mine again.

Dreams in which I dream about my dreams, dreams which remember other dreams: the giant cafeteria in the library in the middle of the maze-like high school, all that eating and reading together. "I dreamed about this, but it's real," I say, before I wake up.

※

Dreams in which my mother isn't dead but only hiding. Her survival is a secret I mustn't tell, she's in danger otherwise. Only I can know that she's alive. I wake up so happy and then I remember.

Dreams in which the black opera singer Jessye Norman slowly promenades over an elaborate stone bridge, wearing a powder-blue gown with a jeweled headdress and an enormous train billowing behind her, singing a stately, soaring aria (reminiscent of Bellini's "Casta Diva"). During the refrain an unseen chorus sings *Ah-ah, pale Gomorrah* over her extended, melismatic vocalise. She looks like some ideal version of my mother.

Dreams in which I write the perfect poem, painstakingly setting down each word, but forget it when I wake up. Dreams in which I wake up and write down the poem I've just dreamed to make sure that I won't forget it, but then I wake up again and realize that I was still dreaming. Sometimes a phrase or a line lingers in my head, and it makes no sense at all.

My sleep is jagged, has sharp edges. I wake as someone I've never been.

Play Dead

Gods envy us because we die, they kill us
out of jealousy, and sometimes
just because they're bored. *When I was
usurped by death* . . . The ghosts roam nude
except for their despair, eyeless
in the underworld, unable to see, to touch,
to taste or hear the world that was so good
when they were too dissatisfied to notice. Hell
is the place the dead who don't know
they're dead go, or where the dead who've always

been dead go when they die in earnest, filled
with small gray flowers that seen up close
are balls of dust. But they don't
see them, though dust clings to them, covers them
like shrouds, if they wore shrouds, if they weren't naked
and dismayed, stripped of whatever made them
whatever they were. Whatever made them whole
has left this hole to call themselves, if they
could call. But they're just shadows
at noon, when shadows are abbreviated, barely

cast. The dead move fast, nowhere
to nowhere in no time at all.

Next Year in Gomorrah

This sentence handed down on a winter beach
by a voice refusing to be anyone's, words
too certain to be merciful
or kind: *No choice is ever pure.* (The voice

is full of distance, sounds like clay,
thick, red, refractory, hard to work through.
It stains the hands and finger
-nails.) As if the wind that shears

the bracken fringes (shaping but refusing
to take shape) had anything but salt
to say: a gift wrapped in acrid fog
that cannot be refused. Salt sees nothing,

says nothing nothing nothing. Evaporation
makes a thick mist on the water, lake and land
breezes leave the lake in all directions
all day long, reverse their course when night

falls upon you. Wind keeps taking place,
repeating salt from lake and shore. Called it
Salt Sea, East Sea, Sea of the Plain. *Guess what
is in this box.* Sea of Lot, they'll call it

in a language no one speaks
yet. The lake's only vegetation is scattered
halophytes that thrive in saline soils, meaning
these tamarisks love you, what you have

become. They fan you with their feathery
pink flower clusters at noon, manna
congeals on their stems. Fish carried in by Jordan
or the smaller streams die instantly,

but this plain spills its fertility
across your Bronze Age riverbanks, lined with
acacias, willows, reeds and white poplars. When is
your now? (Wind keeps repeating meanings of names:

earth; *gazelles* or *roes*; *small*, also
called *a swallowed thing*; *burning*, or
the walled; *submersion*.) Winters
are mild and call you by name,

owing to the lake's low elevation, its sheltered
location. You walk beside the body
of unwritten myth, beside the
lowest body of water on earth, collecting

cowrie shells and lizard skulls, shards of
obsidian and broken ivory pins
turn in your curious fingers. The sea
supports no life, but the fossils

testify. No choice is ever yours, throw the bones
and find your fate. Who wants to know?
Mineral salts, potash and bromine
are commercially extracted, waters

pumped from the shallows into
solar evaporation pans. Of the five
cities of the plain huddled on the sea's
southern shores, only Zoar was spared.

Oh, just pain. You thought the box said "rain,"
rain's scant, seldom graffiti wearing away
whatever's scribbled in the sand. Admah, Zeboiim,
Zoar; your Sodom, your Gomorrah. No choice

is ever sure: the curse of certainty
holds you to a place that once was yours,
sentences you to a single posture, the fossil
of your feelings turning back

from turning away. The past is kept in brine
for you (four cities drowned and preserved),
the lower waters fossilized, the upper waters
your contemporaries. It needn't be

looked back to the way a salt figure
on Mount Sedom overlooks the ashen
beach (the Valley of Siddim, no lower ground
in the world), set nameless in someone else's

history. Waiting beside that absence,
the carapace of fact pulled around
your former self, you take up
so little space. The Dead Sea

———

is an enormous salt reserve, its level
fluctuating throughout the year.

Kings Go Forth

From here it looks like forgiveness,
the possibility of a man: himself a meadow
I traverse by sight, by feel, hand over hand
across the green of him, eyelight by eyelight
until I take him all in. Or is it just the front yard
again, azaleas, hot pepper plants, and a stand
of pampas grass at the border, sweet basil
that's finally given up? He can't be taken in, or not
by me, I lay myself beside him to be almost
so verdant. The wild lantana I uprooted
he replanted, it's flowering for the second time
this year; the adjacent anthill thrums
with its private business. The ants don't interfere
with the numerous small blooms, some
almost pink, some unqualifiedly white; ants
don't distinguish between ornament and weed.

A field of things that can be touched but never owned,
occasional grackles rifling through the undergrowth, or
another's body, for example, his hair
tangled in my fingers momentarily,
each strand as separate as each digit
returning to the hand, and the hand after a moment
to my side. The figure always too consistent,
but capable of raising the hand again, rising to meet
another figure rising too, somewhat like these
palmate leaves rising in an October breeze,
yes, somewhat exactly like the leaves.

Seize the Day

The light in this city is summer
slouched in classic attitudes. It slaps
the face, hunting down a home
in every brick and pore
of the it-won't-stay-for-long, a year
of ghosts forced into fiction. Air's violent
poetry is saturated with salvation
and heavy rains, silt fills the mouth
instead of words, settling into red clay gullies
erosion scrawls down mobile
slopes; black plastic fences try to hold
the roadside in. Presume you, presume
me, forget: the buried rhyme of poverty
and pollution has killed off so many
pollinators, this green butterfly
or moth has followed us from one house
to another, tracing the vanishing margin
of safety: a berm of purple flowers
lines the driveway. The holly bush
makes its complaints known
through thorns on every pointed leaf,
the prevailing local toxins lie
in welcome, make you look through
these lush and poisoned landscapes
for an exit. The texture of evidence
pinched between two fingers
or scratching the passing cheek,
the living grit that scars, illuminates
the war against appearances.
You pause to hear the picture

postcard yards and lawns, listening
at six and then eleven. (News
is a desperate mystery, isn't it,
the paradox of dead light
staining morning air, drenched
in unasked questions.) You learned early
how to tell lies
as if you were human.